THE POOR
WILL BE GLAD

THE POOR WILL BE GLAD

JOINING THE REVOLUTION TO LIFT THE WORLD OUT OF POVERTY

PETER GREER & PHIL SMITH

PHOTOGRAPHY BY JEREMY COWART

ZONDERVAN®

ZONDERVAN.com/
AUTHOR**TRACKER**
follow your favorite authors

ZONDERVAN

The Poor Will Be Glad
Copyright © 2009 by Peter Greer and Phil Smith

This title is also available as a Zondervan ebook. Visit www.zondervan.com/ebooks.

This title is also available in a Zondervan audio edition. Visit www.zondervan.fm.

Requests for information should be addressed to:

Zondervan, *Grand Rapids, Michigan 49530*

Library of Congress Cataloging-in-Publication Data

Greer, Peter, 1975–
    The poor will be glad : joining the revolution to lift the world out of poverty / Peter Greer
and Phil Smith ; with photography by Jeremy Cowart.
       p. cm.
  Includes bibliographical references.
    ISBN 978-0-310-29359-0 (hardcover, jacketed)
    1. Poverty—Religious aspects—Christianity. 2. Church work with the poor. I. Smith, Philip
B. Philip Bartlett) II. Title.
  BV4647.P6G74   2009
  261.8'325—dc22
                                          2009005602

Published in association with the literary agency of Daniel Literary Group, LLC, 1701 Kingsbury Drive, Suite 100, Nashville, TN 37215.

All photographs copyright © Jeremy Cowart.

Interior design by Beth Shagene

Printed in China

09 10 11 12 13 14 15 • 26 25 24 23 22 21 20 19 18 17 16 15 14 13 12 11 10 9 8 7 6 5 4 3 2

TO LAUREL AND SHANNON

CONTENTS

PART III: JOINING THE REVOLUTION

ACRONYMS

AIDS	Acquired immune deficiency syndrome
APR	Annual percentage rate
BAM	Business as Mission
BRI	Bank Rakyat Indonesia
CCT	Center for Community Transformation
CEDI	Christian Economic Development Institution
CFW Shops	Child & Family Wellness Shops
CGAP	Consultative Group to Assist the Poor
CRECER	Credito con Educacion Rural
DRC	Democratic Republic of Congo
GNP	Gross National Product
HIV	Human immunodeficiency virus
HOPE	HOPE International
HUL	Hindustan Unilevel Unlimited
IFAD	International Fund for Agricultural Development
MDG	Millennium development goals
MFI	Microfinance Institution
MIA	Micro Insurance Agency
NGO	Non-Governmental organization
OI	Opportunity International
RoSCA	Rotating Savings & Credit Association
SCA	Savings & Credit Association

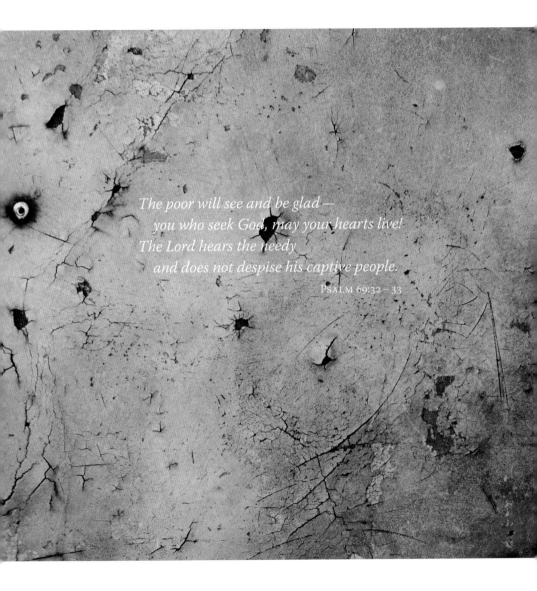

The poor will see and be glad—
    you who seek God, may your hearts live!
The Lord hears the needy
    and does not despise his captive people.

PSALM 69:32–33

FOREWORD
BY ROB BELL

In 2004 I was at a market in Rwanda, watching a woman run her stall. She was selling things and interacting with people, and the whole time she had this huge smile on her face. Someone explained to me that not long ago, this woman had nothing. No food for her family, no home, no money for school for her kids — nothing. She was given a loan as part of a microfinance program. With it she started her business, paid back the loan, built a home that she has no debt on, and now sends her well-fed kids to school. No wonder she was smiling.

I asked how much the loan was for: "Forty American dollars."

Stunning.

And do you know what was done with the $40 when she paid it back? It was loaned to someone else. And then someone else. And then someone else.

Now I assume you're thinking what I first did: What's the catch? What's the scam? It's too good to be true, so it must not be …

Because if it is true and legit and if microfinance really does have that kind of effect on the lives of those in poverty, well, that would change everything.

Which is what it's doing. It's changing things on a massive scale. And every one of us can be a part of it. For a small amount of money, entire families can be empowered to create entirely new tomorrows.

I hope this raises all sorts of questions for you, beginning with: How?

And to answer that question, you'll have to turn the page and start reading this inspiring, informative, moving, world changing, extraordinary book.

GLIMPSES OF POVERTY

We cannot hide from the problem of poverty — it is everywhere. We may cross the street to avoid a homeless man, but that moves us closer to a TV in a storefront window where the eyes of a desperate child in a relief agency's commercial beg us: Do something! Stopping to consider poverty is uncomfortable — it makes us feel guilty. What can one person really do about such an enormous problem or even about one homeless man? It's easy to pretend we don't see and to keep walking.

A new movement is opening our eyes to the reality of poverty around the world. Bono is singing and advocating for the voiceless in sub-Saharan Africa, while Bill and Melinda Gates are pouring massive resources into forgotten regions of the globe. Rick Warren's ambitious Peace Plan is gaining attention, and millions of Christ-followers are working to bring justice, mercy, and lasting compassion to the poorest parts of our world.

The explosion of global short-term missions is challenging the conscience of the American church. More and more of us are beginning to understand that the lifestyle we enjoy in the USA is far from universal. We are the richest of the rich — our complaints about a mall's holiday traffic jams are deeply offensive to our poor brothers and sisters around the world. Hand in hand with this realization is the radical conviction that we need to act. Our faith must change how we live and how we respond to the needs of others — or it will be a faith that James insists is "dead."

The question before the American church is this: How can Christians extend compassion and good intentions into action that makes a lasting difference?

If we understand that Jesus wasn't simply making a polite observation when he said, "From the one who has been entrusted with much, much more will be asked" (Luke 12:48 TNIV), we must ask ourselves what we are doing with our material blessings. How do we serve the poor? How should we?

These are critical questions. Like you, we are deeply concerned about the physical and spiritual poverty in our world. Like you, we are searching for ways that followers of Christ can effectively serve the poor. And, like you, we believe that Jesus' example and the Scriptures have much to teach in this regard.

However, the answers aren't always as clear as the questions. Rebecca Loveless, who works in international ministries at Discovery Church in Orlando, describes the dilemma she faces: "I felt guilty when I wasn't doing anything to help the poor internationally, but after trying a few projects, I now feel guilty as I see that our actions might have actually harmed the people we were trying to help."[1] Rebecca recognizes that taking effective action is not as easy as it might seem. Wise involvement in church-led international ministries could lift millions out of poverty and help build vital local churches in every corner of the globe — but these results are not inevitable simply because there is a surge of excitement.

This book examines how followers of Christ can best counter extreme global poverty. We explore common faults in many Christian-based anti-poverty programs and suggest employment-based solutions with proven results for effectively reducing poverty and extending the kingdom of God. Among these solutions are savings mobilization and microfinance services, which we believe are the most effective methods available to the church in the battle against spiritual and physical poverty.

Allow us to briefly introduce ourselves before we begin to discuss global poverty and its possible solutions.

PETER GREER

Who can forget the white Ford Bronco on every television on June 12, 1994? I was completing my freshman year of college when O. J. Simpson became *the* subject of conversation. Did you see the chase? Would the glove fit? What would Johnny Cochran say next? What I failed to realize was that another, more horrendous event was occurring simultaneously on another continent.

Beginning in April 1994, the small central African country of Rwanda was torn apart by genocide. In only one hundred days, over 800,000 people were brutally murdered in a horrifyingly systematic ethnic cleansing. Until the movie *Hotel Rwanda* brought this event into many comfortable living rooms, it was rare to find someone who really understood what happened.

In 1999 I moved to Rwanda with two suitcases and a desire to help. I was the managing director of Urwego, a Rwandan microfinance institution with the mission of alleviating physical and spiritual poverty through small loans and biblically based business training.[2] In Rwanda, my worldview and my Christian faith were radically reshaped. I was confronted by a level of physical need previously unimaginable to someone who grew up in a comfortable Boston suburb. I was shocked by how little I knew about the genocide and the dehumanizing effects of extreme poverty. Until then, my faith had been sheltered and safe.

How should I respond to the emotional and physical scars of a friend who managed to survive the genocide by nearly submerging herself for days in the feces and urine of a latrine? How could I help a woman who exchanged sex for food to feed her children? What about the seemingly endless number of orphans whose parents were painfully killed by AIDS? What is the good news of Jesus Christ for the millions of people living in poverty? And why isn't the American church doing more to help?

Returning to graduate school at Harvard University provided an extraordinary opportunity to study macroeconomics, econometrics, and economic development. Still, some of my deepest questions remained unanswered. These were questions about how our faith should inform our service and why Jesus kept talking about good news for the poor. As a pastor's kid, I grew up hearing from missionaries who planted churches, yet I saw few models where followers of Jesus Christ met both physical and spiritual needs around the world. Scripture is emphatic about the importance of both; why did the church often seem to neglect physical concerns?

As president of HOPE International, an organization focused on Christ-centered economic development in some of the most challenging places in the world, I have the privilege to seek answers to these vital questions. Through my travels to places ranging from small towns in Haiti to remote villages in northern Afghanistan, I have come to believe three very basic statements about global poverty and our response:

- Poverty in many parts of the world is far worse than most Americans understand, but despite the significant depth and breadth of poverty, the situation is not hopeless.

- Employment and economic development, not handouts, are the most effective and lasting ways of addressing physical and spiritual poverty.

- This is a critical time for the church in America to fight poverty in a way that demonstrates what the church stands *for* and not only what it stands *against*.

Everywhere I look, I see signs pointing toward a new engagement with global poverty. The church is ready for engagement — and all we need is a clear pathway to turn our enthusiasm into actions that will radically impact extreme poverty and bring the love of Christ to the poor. We hope this book helps fuel this rapidly growing movement.

PHIL SMITH

I am probably a lot like you — a Christian trying to do a little better every day. I'm not a preacher, missionary, or the head of an international aid organization. However, my experience as the CEO of two large companies has given me a special perspective on creative business solutions that can be used to help people living in financial destitution.

In 2002 I began trying to understand how to spend the rest of my life doing the "good works, which God prepared in advance for [me] to do" (Ephesians 2:10). For the next five years I involved myself in many charitable activities as I searched for the right fit for my business skills. As a part of my search, I learned about microfinance and began funding projects in countries I never knew existed — I distinctly remember the shock of discovering that Malawi is a country in Africa, not an island in Hawaii! To share what I was learning, I coauthored *A Billion Bootstraps* with Eric Thurman in 2007, a book about microfinance from a donor's perspective that also addresses the broader question of how to give effectively.

But something important was still missing — until I had a life-changing aha! moment. Aha! moments are when your heart aches, your knees quake, and your beliefs shake. They are moments of clarity when the scales fall off your eyes and you see the world in a new way. My moment happened at lunch with Mitch Wilburn, a pastor at a church in the buckle of the Bible Belt — Tulsa, Oklahoma.

Mitch told me about how he'd traveled to Haiti to visit Brad, a friend from college. Brad had been a burly, violent football player during his college years, but he'd experienced his own aha! moment and decided to become a nurse so he could help meet the physical and spiritual needs of poor Haitians, especially babies suffering with HIV and AIDS. Brad helped the community where he lived build a school, a medical clinic, and a church, and he developed new techniques to care for sick children.

With tears in his eyes, Mitch described watching Brad tenderly hold a tiny baby in his massive hands. It was clear this baby would soon die. Mitch asked, "How many dying babies have you held?" Nothing could have prepared him for his crushing aha! moment that followed as Brad met his eyes and replied, "This week?"

Having lunch in that plush country club dining room with Mitch, I was shocked into clarity by Brad's story. No matter how hard I try, there is no way I can truly understand even a fraction of the problems of the world's four billion poor. The comforting words of my faith that I repeat so easily must surely ring hollow to people struggling to find daily food and watching their children die.

This powerful moment caused me to reread the New Testament several times in an effort to understand what the Bible says about helping the disadvantaged and sharing the gospel with them. Easy answers and misconceptions which had long dominated my Christian beliefs began to look less and less like the ones Jesus would have in this day and time.

This book integrates practical information on global poverty with an earnest call to the church to respond quickly, wisely, and compassionately — to be the hands and the voice of God's love. The poor have much to teach our complacent Western church. We need to understand global poverty before we can begin to work on suggestions and solutions. But first, learn how a little girl in India with a fistful of flower petals changed a father's life.

PART I

HOW BAD IS POVERTY ANYWAY?

1

FLOWER PETALS
IN THE FACE

(PETER)

Mumbai, the capital city of India's Maharashtra province, is known as the home of Bollywood films and India's financial capital. In a remote town 150 miles southwest of Mumbai and worlds away from the glitz and glamour of the city, Grace Home Orphanage provides a refuge for abandoned children. When our small group of American visitors arrived, we were welcomed by a line of girls holding handfuls of flower petals. One small girl named Malika[1] emerged from the shadows of the dimly lit doorframe wearing a yellow sari. Instead of gently tossing her flower petals on the ground in front of the visitors as the other girls did, her eyes sparkled as she threw them directly at us! She reminded me of my daughter — the same smile, spunk, and ineffable glow. I couldn't take my eyes off her as she danced with the other girls in a welcome ceremony, accompanied by the beat of Indian drums and the wail of the sitar.

I struggled to understand what a girl like Malika was doing in this orphanage. She should have been dancing at home with her loving parents and siblings, the way things are "supposed to be." Instead, she was one girl out of dozens at this isolated orphanage in India. What circumstances brought her here?

Later that evening we learned that several of these girls had been

"indentured servants" — child slaves, basically — and suffered unspeakable abuse. Their parents were so poor that they saw no options other than selling off one child in order to provide food for the remaining children.

That evening as I tossed and turned beneath my mosquito net, I couldn't help comparing my daughter Liliana and my new friend Malika. Liliana lives in her own room decorated with hanging butterflies, white bunk beds, and pastel pink bedspreads. Malika shares a drab yellow room with twenty-four other girls. Liliana eats three full meals a day that have incredible variety and loves Little Nemo Fruit Snacks in the afternoon, while Malika eats lentil porridge every day and is thankful for the special occasions when she eats meat. Liliana attends Sunday school every week without a thought for her safety. Malika lives in a country where attackers regularly vandalize Christian churches and homes, and threaten, harass, and even kill Indian Christians.[2]

The heartbreaking reality is that these differences are largely the result of one fact: Liliana was born in Pennsylvania, and Malika was born in India. This fact means that my daughter — and nearly every other child born in America — will never face certain evils and injustices that are the daily reality for hundreds of millions of children in the world.

Hunger: Liliana will never go to bed hungry unless she refuses to eat her broccoli and her mother and I are trying to teach her an important lesson. In developing countries, approximately 850 million people go to bed hungry every night and search for creative ways to ignore their discomfort. Andrew Samuel, a banker who grew up in India, remembers his mother telling him to sleep on his stomach because it helped quell hunger pains.

Child Mortality: It is highly unlikely that Liliana will experience the pain of losing a brother or sister before she reaches elementary school. In Angola, almost one in five children dies during childbirth. Worldwide, eleven million children die every year before reaching their fifth birthday. That translates to thirty thousand children who die each day from hunger and preventable disease — one child every three seconds.[3]

Drinking Water: Liliana can drink directly from a faucet at one of the four sinks in our home without any concern for her health. Twenty percent of the world has no access to clean water. Millions more walk long distances to carry every drop of water to their homes.

Toilets and Diarrhea: Liliana has access to indoor plumbing and considers diarrhea a temporary inconvenience. In the developing world, diarrhea wracks the thin bodies of tens of millions of children who have no access to diapers or plumbing — and it kills between 1.6 and 2.5 million children every year.[4]

Education: Liliana will attend our city's public schools for free and already knows her letters. In the least developed countries, the literacy rate is 51 percent.[5] In Afghanistan the female literacy rate is 12 percent, and most women are not educated beyond the fourth grade.[6]

Health Care: Liliana dislikes the pain of routine shots provided by her doctor. More than half of all Africans do not have access to modern health facilities.[7] The result is ten million annual deaths from the four most common preventable diseases: diarrhea, acute respiratory illness, malaria, and measles. In many cases, one simple shot could save a life.

Life Expectancy: If statistical models are correct, Liliana will live past the age of eighty.[8] If she were born in Swaziland, she wouldn't expect to live much past the age of thirty.[9]

Washing Machine and a Change of Clothes: Liliana's mother and I wash her clothes easily in a washing machine and choose her clothes from a

dresser full of pants and shirts. In other parts of the world, children — and often their mothers — must hand wash every item of clothing, a labor- and time-intensive task. When a friend gave a T-shirt to a boy in Zambia, the boy's grateful response was, "Now when I wash my shirt, I do not have to be naked when it dries."

Women's Rights: My daughter will have to overcome certain biases because she is a woman. But these hurdles pale by comparison to the experience of so many others in the developing world. An Afghan man was told that his sick daughter's life could be saved if he took her across a dangerous mountain pass to medical care in a city two hours away. "No, I don't want to do that," he responded. "Girls are free, but donkeys cost money."[10]

Employment: On my way to work today, I passed at least a dozen businesses with "Help Wanted" signs, many of which would be happy to hire Liliana if she were sixteen. In the Democratic Republic of the Congo, only 10 percent of the *entire population* is formally employed. There simply are no formal employment options, no "Help Wanted" signs, and no employers who are legally mandated to provide a minimum wage and other rights.

Financial Services: Liliana and I will open a savings account at our local branch of Graystone Bank when she turns five. Such an account would be an unimaginable luxury in much of the world. In several countries, fewer than one in a thousand has access to a safe place to begin saving money. Fewer still have any way of accessing reasonably priced credit to begin a small business or to cover the expenses of an emergency.

The reality is that the scale of poverty in the developing world dwarfs nearly everything we label as "poor" in the United States. This is exceptionally difficult for most Americans to understand, including me. Growing up, I was the "poor pastor's kid" in a wealthy Boston suburb. When everyone else had Nintendos, I had hand-me-down Ataris. How naïve I was — and many of us still are — to equate slightly less luxury with the dehumanizing struggle to survive that confronts the nearly three billion people who try to survive on less than $2 a day.

Poverty in America is still a very real problem. Events like Hurricane Katrina remind us of just how many Americans are without an adequate safety net, not to mention daily necessities. However, the vast majority of poverty in America is "defined poverty" or "relative poverty." If "poor" is defined as the 10 percent of the people in a nation earning the lowest income, then 10 percent of that nation will always be "poor" no matter how many resources they have. Without suggesting that the pain of those who are poor in America should be ignored, it is a fact that most poor people in the United States have astounding resources when compared to those in the developing world.[11]

A December 2005 article in *The Economist* treated this issue by comparing the lives of Dr. Mbwebwe Kabamba, a prominent surgeon in Kinshasa, the capital of the Democratic Republic of the Congo, and Enos Banks, an unemployed coal driver in eastern Kentucky's Appalachia region. Both men live on nearly the same amount of money, yet there are significant differences in their lifestyles. Dr. Kabamba has no running water at his house, has the benefits from electricity twice a week, only dreams of air conditioning, and eats meat about twice a month. In the America of Enos Banks, three quarters of poor households have air conditioning and the poor eat more meat than the well-to-do. On average, poor people in America are likely to live longer than the poor in other countries, spend more years in education, have jobs, and own cars, refrigerators, stereos, and other luxuries. The article summarizes: "All one can say is that whereas the poor in Kinshasa complain about the price of bread, the poor in Kentucky complain about the price of motor insurance ... If poor Americans were to compare their standard of living with what is normal elsewhere in the world, let alone in Congo, they would see they have little cause for discontent."[12]

The poor in America live at an economic level far above the poor in other parts of the world. If you had the choice of being born into a poor family in the United States or a poor family in Congo, which would you

choose? For that matter, would you rather be born into a poor family in the United States or a *wealthy* family in Congo? There is no question that the poor in America have much greater security, opportunity, and provision when compared to developing countries.

Let us reiterate: it is not our intention to suggest that the poor in America suffer no pain or hardship or that the church should not be helping the poor in our own cities. Rather, we wish to emphasize the extreme and immediate needs of the poor in developing countries. There are people who literally struggle to survive *every day of their lives.* The extent of this global poverty is staggering. As of July 2007, there were approximately 6.6 billion people living on earth. Approximately four billion live on less than $4 per day, nearly all of whom live in developing countries. Their incomes are distributed in the following way:

- One billion live on less than $1 per day.
- Two billion live on $1 to $2 per day.
- One billion live on $2 to $4 per day.[13]

The wealthy, and that includes everyone reading this book, lead lives that many of the four billion people living on less than $4 per day consider an unreachable dream.[14]

WHAT NOW?

Ruth Callanta, founder of the Center for Community Transformation in the Philippines, wondered, "Why do we live in a place that has so much and yet there are so many poor? Are there not enough fish in the sea? Does the earth not have the capacity to provide sufficient food? This cannot be what God has planned for His creation. Something is definitely wrong."[15]

Something *is* wrong. But in the haze of desperation and despair, hope is breaking through. The church is beginning to combat extreme poverty in a new way. This movement is radically different from traditional charity. It focuses on long-term systemic change and lasting employment patterns, not short-term quick fixes. It emphasizes the importance of partnerships and local champions, not external "saviors" descending to solve the problems of the poor. The hope of the gospel is integrated through tangible acts of compassion that have long-term reach, rather than simply providing handouts that keep the poor in a position of dependency.

This is the beginning of a new movement led by microfinance ministries, where small loans and local relationships are used to bring lasting change to poor communities. The revolution has begun.

2

MAKING A FEAST FOR JESUS

(PHIL)

Three out of four ways the church tries to share the gospel will fail to have long-term results. I think Jesus implies as much in the parable of the soils (Matthew 13:3 – 23). So we shouldn't be surprised when money and effort spent on sharing the good news often seem to have little long-term benefit. There are two choices: continue to do the same things over and over and expect different results (which is one definition of insanity), or imitate the example in another parable and change the way we do things. In Luke 13:6 – 9, Jesus tells of a worker who wasn't content to have soil conditions that would result in an unproductive tree. He took the initiative to change the soil by digging and fertilizing. Isn't it time to consider modifying some of our past methods in an attempt to improve our effectiveness of sharing the gospel with the whole world?

As we consider gospel-sharing efforts in the developing world, we are immediately faced with an issue that cannot be ignored: how much of the church's precious resources should be used to contend with the genuine problem of poverty?

Since Jesus said, "The poor you will always have with you" (Matthew 26:11), isn't attempting to alleviate poverty a pointless task, like pouring water down a drain? Besides, isn't a healthy portion of the money we pay in taxes funding the massive amounts of aid America sends to developing countries? Wouldn't working to end poverty distract the church from its mission of proclaiming salvation in Jesus Christ? And doesn't it seem like the church should be focused on achievable goals — like saving souls — rather than a utopian social dream?

My understanding of poverty and the church's proper response began to change at home in my favorite room — the kitchen. My wife, Shannon, is a professional chef who loves teaching youngsters how to cook. Peeking into the kitchen recently, I saw my daughter and three other girls cooking. Meredith was chopping onions with sunglasses on to keep her eyes from watering, while Hanna was tentatively cutting carrots, and the two other girls were working at their own assigned tasks. Under Shannon's tutelage, these teenagers were making a feast of roasted pepper pork with raspberry sauce, garlic potatoes, and fresh sautéed green beans.

As I walked back to my office, it hit me. Meredith wasn't just mechanically chopping onions; she was making a *feast*. Hanna wasn't just cutting carrots; she was preparing a *banquet*. With a common purpose, recipes, and teamwork, the girls were creating something greater and more beautiful than the sum of its parts. While you can chop vegetables without making a feast, you can't make a feast without chopping vegetables.

Sitting in my office, I thought about the church's stance on international poverty and missions. "What are we making?" I wondered. "A feast or just a mountain of carrot sticks?" There are Christians doing millions of tasks around the world every day. We give away wheelchairs, start orphanages, pass out bags of rice, and dig wells. We proclaim the gospel, teach in theological institutions, and plant churches.

Surely all these activities are "good," but how do they join together in making a savory feast? What is the recipe that should unite the efforts of the church? Here is the key question — is serving the poor a distraction from our "core" mission of evangelism and discipleship or is it a necessary ingredient? Jesus said, "People will come from east and west and north and south, and will take their places at the feast in the kingdom of God" (Luke 13:29). As we consider how to do our part in making the feast and increasing the number of invitees to it, let's explore the biblical and historical background of service to the poor and examine its contemporary relevance.

A PARADOX

For the first fifty years of my life, I didn't recognize one of the paradoxes in my thought process. Most churches I attended had a missions committee focused on evangelism and a benevolence committee responsible for giving to the poor. This structure separated proclaiming the gospel from meeting physical needs. Church members seemed to internalize the message that the two functions were separate.

Missions committees were motivated and directed by Scriptures such as, "Therefore go and make disciples of all nations, baptizing them in the name of the Father and of the Son and of the Holy Spirit, and teaching them to obey everything I have commanded you" (Matthew 28:19 – 20); "But you will receive power when the Holy Spirit comes on you; and you will be my witnesses in Jerusalem, and in all Judea and Samaria, and to the ends of the earth" (Acts 1:8); "And how can they hear without someone preaching to them? And how can they preach unless they are sent? As it is written, 'How beautiful are the feet of those who bring good news!'" (Romans 10:14 – 15). With these Scriptures in mind, the missions committees spent their budgets primarily on sending American missionaries overseas or to isolated American communities.

Benevolence committees were motivated by Scriptures such as: "I tell you the truth, whatever you did for one of the least of these brothers of mine, you did for me" (Matthew 25:40); "Sell everything you have and give to the poor, and you will have treasure in heaven" (Luke 18:22); and "Suppose a brother or sister is without clothes and daily food. If one of you says to him, 'Go, I wish you well; keep warm and well fed,' but does nothing about his physical needs, what good is it?" (James 2:15 – 16). Heeding these words, they feed the hungry, clothe the naked, and shelter the homeless. Most often this occurs in the local community, but sometimes it is done overseas too.

The acts of meeting spiritual needs and physical needs are so often separated that many Christians no longer seem to notice. The following chart is a useful gauge of your own view of the church's mission and per-

	LOW EMPHASIS ON DEED	HIGH EMPHASIS ON DEED
LOW EMPHASIS ON WORD		
HIGH EMPHASIS ON WORD		

haps of the way you were raised. Where would you place yourself and your local church? Do you tend to emphasize the proclamation of the good news of Jesus Christ or to live out your faith through acts of compassion and service?

How does Scripture lead us in thinking through this issue? Let's examine the life of Christ and the response of the early church.

THE EXAMPLE OF JESUS

In Luke 4:16 – 30, Jesus publicly declares his mandate on earth for the first time. He is speaking to people who think they know him, yet his words produce a murderous fury. What could have been so inflammatory?

Jesus first reads from the Old Testament passage of Isaiah 61:1 – 2: "The Spirit of the Lord is on me, because he has anointed me to preach good news to the poor. He has sent me to proclaim freedom for the prisoners and recovery of sight for the blind, to release the oppressed, to proclaim the year of the Lord's favor" (Luke 4:18 – 19). Jesus takes those familiar words and startles his listeners with his one-point sermon: "Today this scripture is fulfilled in your hearing" (v. 21). He goes on to say these benefits will extend to those outside of the Jewish faith.

When Jesus spoke of "the year of the Lord's favor," he was probably referring to the year of Jubilee. Every fifty years a trumpet was blown on the Day of Atonement to "proclaim liberty throughout the land to all its inhabitants" (Leviticus 25:10). This proclamation freed people from crushing debt and slavery and returned land to families who had been forced by economic hardship to sell it. Jubilee alleviated the worst effects of continuing indebtedness and poverty; it was the release from debt and the restoration of rightful inheritance.

This way of describing Jesus' mission has both concrete and spiritual dimensions. The word *release* in Greek, Aramaic, and Hebrew means breaking free from financial debts as well as the release from or forgiveness

of sins. God is concerned about economic realities, physical imprisonment, and visual blindness, but he also speaks of freedom from the debt of sin and spiritual bondage.

Jesus lived this full definition of release by combining care for the physical person with care for the soul. From the beginning, "Jesus went throughout Galilee, teaching in their synagogues, preaching the good news of the kingdom, and healing every disease and sickness among the people" (Matthew 4:23). He both proclaimed and demonstrated freedom in its most complete sense.

At the start of Jesus' ministry, John the Baptist sent two of his men to Jesus with this question: "Are you the one who was to come, or should we expect someone else?" As Luke tells the story in Luke 7:18 – 23, it appears

Jesus heard the question and, without saying a word, turned away and continued whatever he was already doing. After a time, Jesus sent the two men back to John with instructions to tell him what they had seen and heard: "The blind receive sight, the lame walk, those who have leprosy are cured, the deaf hear, the dead are raised, and the good news is preached to the poor" (v. 22). When Jesus specifically sets out to prove that he is the Messiah, the Promised One, what does he do? He meets the physical needs of people *and* preaches good news to the poor.

There were times when Jesus taught and other times he simply met people's physical needs. In each situation, he did what best demonstrated the dual nature of the kingdom of God — that it will last for eternity and is already here changing lives. Rather than viewing the actions and teachings of Jesus as a rainbow spectrum of loving and necessary interactions, we often separate the colors with a distorted prism because we want to emphasize one thing or another. Perhaps we have a personal preference for spoken evangelism or for fighting physical hunger, but our preferences should not place filters before our eyes and cause us to ignore the balance that's so evident in the life of Christ.

A clear example of an unfiltered viewpoint is the interplay between the Great Commission and the Greatest Commandment. Not long before departing the earth, Jesus commissioned his disciples, saying, "Therefore go and make disciples of all nations, baptizing them in the name of the Father and of the Son and of the Holy Spirit, and teaching them to obey everything I have commanded you" (Matthew 28:19 – 20).

Yet only a few weeks earlier, Jesus had given the Greatest Commandment by stating, "'Love the Lord your God with all your heart and with all your soul and with all your mind.' This is the first and greatest commandment. And the second is like it: 'Love your neighbor as yourself'" (Mathew 22:37 – 39). The ministry of Christ demonstrated the seamless harmony of obeying both the Great Commission and the Greatest Commandment.

THE EARLY DISCIPLES

Immediately following the death and resurrection of Jesus Christ, his followers imitated his pattern of meeting both physical and spiritual needs.[1] They understood the ministry of Jesus was to be continued on earth through them by the power of the Holy Spirit. The disciples did not separate doing good works from proclaiming the good news. The gospel wasn't only an abstract idea that could "save souls" but tangible good news with earthly relevance. This had been impressed on the disciples not only by the daily actions of Jesus but in their first assignments.

When Jesus sent out the twelve apostles, and later when he sent out the seventy disciples, his instructions focused on two things: preaching the good news *and* meeting physical needs. Their results were so astounding, Jesus said, "I saw Satan fall like lightning from heaven" (Luke 10:18).

Many years later, the concern of James, Peter, and John that the poor be included in the ongoing proclamation of Christ's message prompted them to encourage Paul to "continue to remember the poor." Paul's response was that this was "the very thing I was eager to do" (Galatians 2:10). That may seem an unlikely response from the apostle so well known for his theological writings that focus on orthodoxy (a proper understanding of who God is). Yet Paul was just as concerned about orthopraxis (right living) and how faith impacts the way we serve others.

For Paul, a proper understanding of what God does for us should change the way we live, including how we interact with the poor. The most successful church established by Paul was in Ephesus. The Ephesian church changed the culture of its city and swelled to as many as fifty thousand members. Acts 19 shows Paul's progress and influence there. He first tried to take the gospel to the Jews in that city. After limited success, he started the first Christian college. In just two years, Paul may have lectured more than four thousand hours in the school, but he did more than just preach the good news: "God did extraordinary miracles through Paul, so that even handkerchiefs and aprons that had touched him were taken to the sick, and their illnesses were cured and the evil spirits left them" (Acts 19:11 – 12).

In Paul's last meeting with the elders of Ephesus, he emphasized the importance of both sharing the gospel directly and meeting physical needs. He said, "However, I consider my life worth nothing to me, if only I may finish the race and complete the task the Lord Jesus has given me — the task of testifying to the gospel of God's grace" (Acts 20:24). He continued, "In everything I did, I showed you that by this kind of hard work we must help the weak, remembering the words the Lord Jesus himself said: 'It is more blessed to give than to receive'" (Acts 20:35).

Paul, perhaps the church's most influential theologian, knew followers of Christ were called to an integrated life. There is no question that throughout the New Testament, the apostles and other leaders were intent on meeting both the spiritual and physical needs of others, just as Jesus was. In the following centuries, early Christians were intent on doing the same.

THE EARLY CHURCH

Rodney Stark argues persuasively in *The Rise of Christianity* that Christianity rose to prominence in the Roman world during the first three centuries after Jesus, because Christians met the physical and spiritual needs of people even during times of plague and suffering.[2] He says the obscure Jewish sect became a dominant religious force as a result of its social benefits. In times of crisis, Christians loved all people, not just "their own." The early centuries of Christianity were trying and difficult times, and epidemics were rampant. Out of fear of catching these illnesses, unbelievers often fled outbreaks, while Christians stayed behind to provide care for those in need. As a result, many unbelievers — who had been essentially abandoned by their previous social networks — converted to Christianity. The doctrines of the Christian faith suddenly made sense to people because they saw that the everyday practice of those doctrines produced a better life. Consequently, Christian community was something for which many people longed.

Christianity grew because it was attractive and inclusive. When suffering people received the love of a Christian community, they often wanted to be a part of that community. While the early Christians still longed for the rewards of heaven, they experienced the blessings of God in their day-to-day lives as well.

Due to the influence of Constantine in the fourth century CE, the Roman Catholic Church became the dominant repository of Christian life in the Western world. Its history of meeting spiritual and physical needs since then is uneven, but certainly there have been leaders of great compassion, such as St. Francis of Assisi, who is believed to have said, "Preach always, use words if necessary." After the Reformation, many Protestant

leaders, such as John Wesley, had an integrated ministry of helping people both spiritually and physically.

EIGHTEENTH- AND NINETEENTH-CENTURY CHRISTIANS

In eighteenth- and nineteenth-century England and America, the pattern of engagement with social concerns remained an unmistakable companion for the message of Christ. One historian said that this period, known as the Evangelical Revival, "did more to transfigure the moral character of the general populace than any other movement British history can record."[3]

The Clapham Sect, including its famous leader William Wilberforce, emerged from this Evangelical Revival. The members of this group were primarily influential Anglicans who showed the power of a ministry in which proclamation and demonstration were inseparable. They were instrumental in founding missionary and tract societies, including the British and Foreign Bible Society and the Church Missionary Society. They also worked tirelessly to combat injustices and establish righteousness throughout the world. Their efforts centered on the liberation of slaves, the abolition of the slave trade both in Britain and around the world, and the reform of the penal system. As celebrated by the movie *Amazing Grace*, the year 2006 marked the bicentennial of the abolition of the slave trade in England, the best known of their efforts.

During this time, there were many other groups and individuals who combined word and deed as they battled social evils around the world, such as the opium trade, forced labor, kidnapping, prostitution, the caste system, and infanticide. Missionaries were as well known for their help in medicine, clean water, and agriculture as for their sharing of the gospel. Nevius introduced the modern orchard industry into Shantung. The Basel missionaries revolutionized the economy of Ghana by introducing coffee and cocoa grown by families and individuals on their own land. James McKean transformed the life of northern Thailand by helping eliminate its three major curses — smallpox, malaria, and leprosy. Wells and pure water, which helped eliminate many illnesses, often came through the help of missionaries. Throughout the nineteenth century, missionaries stressed the importance of industrial schools; from there industries were established.[4]

If the biblical and historical Christian response to poverty is a unified emphasis on the good news and good deeds, why doesn't there seem to be the same level of integration in the efforts of the American church today?

GREAT REVERSALS

As the Evangelical Revival swept through America and England, many church leaders tended to have a strong emphasis on just preaching and converting people. A reversal occurred, according to historian Timothy L. Smith in *Revivalism and Social Reform*, when many Christians wanted to concentrate primarily on social needs they believed were being neglected.

For instance, Walter Rauschenbusch, a leader of the Social Gospel movement in the early 1900s, practiced a faith that addressed poverty and injustice, maintaining that a kingdom of God that is abstracted into some heavenly afterlife is worthless in the slums. "The Kingdom of God is the Christian transfiguration of the social order," Rauschenbusch wrote in 1917 in *A Theology of the Social Gospel*.[5] Such Christians devoted their lives to transforming the earth into a kingdom of God with no poverty or social injustice.

During this time, Christians and their leaders were also being exposed to the intellectual challenges of Darwinism and secular humanism. For many of these people, the desire to share the "old time religion" receded further and further, while emphasis on dealing with people in the here and now became dominant.

Such an emphasis on the physical reality of the kingdom meant, in some cases, a near exclusion of the spiritual realm. A purely social message missed key points about the eternal nature of the kingdom of God and the gospel. This inevitably sparked a backlash and another reversal from Christians concerned with recovering the spiritual and eternal elements of Christ's message. These believers stressed faith over works and evangelism over relief, and so the pendulum swung back — often much too far! Many in the church dismissed the social demands of the gospel entirely, going instead to the opposite extreme of focusing entirely on the spiritual. As the two camps polarized, an integrated approach to the ministry of word and deed became harder to grasp.

The growing evangelical movements in the early 1900s illustrated this change as their emphasis on teaching and preaching seemed to portray these as the only ministries worthy of the church's time and attention. As one example of that legacy, consider the curriculum of the vast majority of evangelical seminaries — the focus is overwhelmingly on teaching and preaching, and there are few courses devoted to finding innovative and meaningful ways to minister physically to people.

As this shift in emphasis occurred, the primary concern for many Christians became "saving souls" and "going to heaven." Over time, Americans — both Christian and otherwise — often acquired the understanding that the singular role of Christianity is to arrive at heaven's gate and to be allowed entry. Although that is certainly something to anticipate with joy, it ignores Jesus' clear, integrated teaching that God's kingdom exists on earth as well. We are instructed to be simultaneously citizens of a future kingdom and ambassadors in this time and place. While we wait for a future with Christ, we are called to do everything we can to bring elements of that glorious future into this world. Jesus talked often about a kingdom that is breaking into this world right now, a kingdom that isn't marked by opulent buildings but by opulent acts of compassion and kindness. This kingdom isn't characterized by its military might but by its willingness to kneel down in selfless service.

The tendency to separate word and deed was subtly influenced by changes in public schools. In the first half of the twentieth century, it was common for American public schools to teach passages from the Bible and to have prayer. By the end of the twentieth century, Christianity was virtually banned from the public school system, while science and human reason became the standard. Modern education is one of the reasons Westerners, including Christians, often separate their spiritual and physical lives. If something can be touched, seen, heard, smelled, or tasted, it belongs to the realm of science. If it can be bought or sold, it belongs in the domain of economics and finance. If it is a matter of faith, it belongs to God — mostly on Sunday. So, from that perspective, loving God is spiritual work, but loving neighbors takes place in the material and economic world.

Bryant L. Myers, a leading voice for Christian engagement with poverty, summarizes this divisive situation:

> So evangelism (restoring people's relationship with God) is spiritual work, while social action (restoring just economic, social, and political relationships among people) is not. In the final analysis this false dichotomy leads Christians to believe that God's redemptive work takes place only in the spiritual realm, while the world is left, seemingly, to the devil.... Because we have tended to accept the dichotomy between the spiritual and the physical, we sometimes inadvertently limit the scope of both sin and the gospel.[6]

GOVERNMENT SHOULD CARE FOR THE POOR, RIGHT?

The church's response to the poor in the United States has also been affected by the increased involvement of our federal and state governments in social programs.[7] The social programs instituted to overcome the devastation of the Great Depression, which included Social Security, the G.I. Bill, and other programs following World War II; the Great Society social bills of the 1960s; and many other massive pieces of legislation have created a social safety net. Without commenting on the efficiency or effectiveness of these programs, we can observe that they further removed the American church from the job of engaging poverty and other social injustices. The work of addressing physical needs was increasingly seen as government work, while the church increased its focus on the spiritual realm.

AN UNHELPFUL DICHOTOMY

Modern thought encourages us to think in hierarchical categories. The word *priority* is an illustration of this. Christian organizations, when considering how to budget their time and money, often develop a list of priorities based on the Bible. However, using the Bible to develop a list of priorities — where number one is more important than number two, and so on — is not a biblical concept. While the Bible speaks often of integrated responsibilities (e.g., faith and works) and tensions (e.g., the kingdom is both already and not yet here), the concept of priority was developed more than a thousand years after the Bible was written. Focusing on the top of a priority list can cause us to miss the full picture of what God desires for us.

Consider how the end of the Great Commission passage

in Matthew 28:19–20 is often interpreted. Jesus said, "Therefore go and make disciples of all nations, baptizing them in the name of the Father and of the Son and of the Holy Spirit, and teaching them to obey everything I have commanded you." In many instances, this teaching is understood to refer exclusively to *propositional evangelism.* Yet Jesus had something far greater in mind: to follow everything he taught with his words and *with his life.* This passage should point believers toward the ministry model of Jesus, who seamlessly integrated proclamation and practice in his ministry to all people, with special attention paid to the poor and downtrodden.

A WAY FORWARD

Based on Scripture and history, I believe church-based programs are most effective when they simultaneously meet both spiritual and physical needs in a culturally appropriate manner. As we will discuss later, to accomplish this, it might be the case that multiple people and organizations need to work side by side without competition or jealousy. If an integrated approach to making disciples is a scriptural imperative, followers of Christ are not at liberty to choose between proclaiming Christ or serving the needs of the world. While this fact may cause discomfort for Christians for a variety of reasons, we should ultimately rejoice in the many advantages of integrated ministry. Here are a few:

- *Integration Increases Effectiveness.* The effectiveness of physical ministry and the effectiveness of verbal ministry are each enhanced when done together.[8]

- *Integration Reenergizes the Church.* American Christians can rightly be accused of being too inwardly focused. Service is what the church was designed for, and when we do it, we benefit in many ways.

- *Integration Helps Correct an Image Problem.* Christians are often known only for what we are against. Helping people materially provides a way for followers of Jesus to be known for something positive. Leroy Barber, president of Mission Year, lays down the gauntlet: "Christian rhetoric without tangible acts of love is hypocrisy."[9]

- *Integration Improves Trust and Builds Relationships.* Research shows that the majority of Christians came to faith as the result of a relationship.[10] Although not supported by rigorous data analysis, my own experience certainly supports the finding that relationships are the most important factor in people coming to faith.

God's body on earth — the church — is uniquely able to provide a special feast for people around the world by simultaneously meeting spiritual and physical needs. Many of the church's characteristics that allow it to function so well in this regard are obvious, such as its physical presence in so many communities around the world. But God provided some additional strategies for the church to use. Charity is one of those strategies that is not only biblically recommended but is relatively easy to use. Unfortunately, it also can be easily misused.

3

SEARCHING FOR SOLUTIONS THAT WORK

(PETER)

When the Soviet Union disintegrated in 1991, the physical and spiritual needs in this broken part of the world became evident. Members of a church in Lancaster County, Pennsylvania, asked, "How can we help?" Through the Slavic Gospel Association, they partnered with a church in Zaporozhye, Ukraine, a city of a million people straddling a river in the country's southeast. This was not a distant, impersonal partnership that amounted to sending an annual check. The church leadership and congregation of Lancaster's Calvary Monument Bible Church (CMBC) considered this a true relationship and wanted to find ways of supporting their brothers and sisters overseas. Just as important, they wanted to be supported by them in a mutually encouraging relationship.

After an initial assessment trip, the leaders at Calvary Monument identified immediate needs and responded. Recognizing that local food production and distribution were inadequate, they shipped food from Lancaster, a region of fertile farmland. They saw that the Ukrainians wore old clothes often insufficient for the harsh winters. Following Jesus' command that if you have two tunics you should give one away, they shared their clothes with their Ukrainian friends. Hospitals and infirmaries in Zaporozhye had little or no supplies, so CMBC arranged for shipments of medicine and medical supplies donated by area doctors and hospitals. They saw that the Ukrainian believers had only a crowded building in which to worship, so they helped purchase land and provide funds to build additional educational space. This pattern continued for several years, marked annually by a special Thanksgiving offering and shipping container filled with food, clothing, and church supplies. CMBC did everything it could think of to help the church in Zaporozhye, and it was not alone; dozens of other American churches developed relationships with churches throughout the former Soviet Union at this pivotal time in history.

CMBC's response was admirable; it was based on relationship, was responsive to seen needs, and was generous. But, paradoxically, it was also flawed.

What was wrong? Shouldn't we celebrate such acts of generosity? Shouldn't we encourage many *more* churches to give sacrificially? Before answering these hard questions, we need to continue the story and watch how the relationship between the Lancaster church and the Ukrainian church developed.

After three years of this "partnership," leaders from both sides of the Atlantic Ocean came to the realization that the help from the American church was, at best, insufficient. The Ukrainian church would *always* have "needs" that the American church could respond to — no amount of giving would change the socioeconomic reality of life in the former Soviet Union.

At worst, the seemingly admirable American support could be harming the Ukrainians. The pastor of the church in Ukraine initially thought it was a blessing to receive generous gifts and support from a church that had no previous ties to his country or people. But he grew increasingly concerned about how this relationship was changing his congregation. He wanted to find a way for his church to become self-sustaining rather that reliant upon distant generosity. He feared his church was becoming increasingly dependent on outside resources and was losing the motivation to serve each other. Why sacrifice anything to feed or clothe a neighbor when an international shipment would soon arrive?

The Ukrainian pastor had other important questions too: What would happen if the generous people in Pennsylvania suddenly stopped providing? Would this kind of assistance produce a stronger community long after the donations stopped? How could the church continue distributing the supplies to the most needy?

There were economic repercussions as well. After more investigation, this pastor determined that the well-intentioned generosity of the Lancaster church would likely hurt the incomes of local businesses which competed with the free American goods and services entering their marketplace.

It seemed the gifts from America, however well-intentioned, might cause more problems than they solved. Both churches were learning a difficult lesson: Compassionate responses to certain needs work well in the short term but are insufficient for the long term. Effective obedience to the clear biblical command to clothe the naked and give food to the hungry requires asking the question of *how*. Thoughtless responses run the real risk of strengthening the chains of poverty that bind captives around the world.

These are hard words for the American church to hear. The experience of CMBC is not unique. More and more American churches are seeking meaningful ways to serve their brothers and sisters around the world. The convenience and affordability of travel have exposed churchgoers from the United States to formerly unknown people and places. We feel compelled to help. The shock of seeing severe poverty has a way of confronting us with how much we have and how protected we are. This emotional reaction — we have to do *something!* — is a wonderful place to start but an insufficient, and possibly even harmful, place to end.

What makes the story of the Lancaster church somewhat unusual is that some of its members were prepared to respond with their hearts *and* their heads.[1] They didn't let their urge to be compassionate stifle their need to ask and listen to tough questions. They were ready to offer an integrated, correctable response to the issue of poverty. The church leaders recognized that unintended and even unimagined consequences always follow actions. We will tell you the ending to this story in chapter 15.

Consequences are seldom discussed at church functions. After a presentation from a team that just handed out food and clothing on a short-term mission trip, who wants to be the pessimist that points out the potential problems of this act of kindness? Imagine responding to a child's excitement about missions with a statement like, "But what unintended impact will our actions have on the local people and marketplace?" Many would be offended by your challenge to their good intentions. When a church body sincerely pours itself into a service project, nobody wants to doubt the results or imagine there could be negative consequences. Yet the detrimental effects of some of the most minor and well-meaning actions are more common than people want to believe.[2]

There are common pitfalls that trap our churches and organizations when they fight global poverty. It is important to take a serious look at successes and failures and honestly evaluate if our efforts leave communities better off than before our "service."

DEPENDENCY AND DISINCENTIVES

In 2005, I went to Afghanistan with a group of donors, pastors, and development practitioners and had the once-in-a-lifetime experience of touring northern Afghanistan in a Russian-made helicopter. We were welcomed into small towns and villages that had not visibly been touched by the outside world.

I particularly remember one tiny mountain village where we were paraded around by local elders who showed us all their "needs." They brought us to a community center that had some minor water damage to the roof. Outside this building, an elder waved his finger at me, saying, "You must fix this!" Now I'm not particularly handy, yet even I could have repaired this small problem with locally available materials and a few hours of sweat. The attitude in that village was that foreigners should be responsible for meeting every need.

Outside assistance had weakened and begun to paralyze local initiative and ownership. As we lifted off, my mind was racing as swiftly as the rotor blades above my head. Surely there must be a better way for believers to participate in addressing the incredible needs in our world.

The attitudes of dependency and disincentive are human — they plague our daily decisions and large-scale development efforts with equal ease. Last year, I heard through the grapevine — okay, my wife spilled the beans — that my in-laws were going to buy me a new watch for Christmas. My watch was on the fritz and I had to keep tapping it to encourage the second hand to move. Knowing a new watch was coming, there was no way I would spend my own money on a new one, and, crucially, there was *no incentive* to bother fixing it either. In fact, solving the problem myself would have been an act of foolishness in this circumstance.

We perpetuate a terrible lie when we say that individuals living in poverty are "too poor to do anything." Each of us has something to give and some responsibility to use our resources and skills to serve.

Misguided giving can actually rob the poor — not of their physical resources, but of their dignity, responsibility, and self-worth. We cannot afford to waste limited resources that could equip and enable people to rebuild their lives, churches, and communities.

Joel Wickre, a board member of Blood:Water Mission, warns about how bad the problem can become:

> People who are treated as helpless come to hold a lesser view of themselves. People who believe they are "blessed to be a blessing" and not in need themselves come to a lesser view of the people they serve. These victim and savior complexes create a co-dependency that perpetuates the problems of poverty and far outweighs any temporary

relief such missions provide.... Poor people understand that getting help requires appearing helpless, and rich people unwittingly advance the helplessness of those they serve by seeing them as objects of charity, not equals.[3]

IMPROPER DIAGNOSIS

A few months ago, my grandmother fell ill and was hospitalized. For two weeks, doctors watched over her and ran a battery of tests until they finally discovered she had a medical condition related to her nervous system. Only at this point was it possible to start proper treatment.

The same principle of diagnosis is true for believers involved in overseas projects. How much time is spent diagnosing the causes before imposing solutions? How much time is spent listening to the people we are seeking to serve and developing strong enough relationships so that we can hear their voices? This model of diagnosis does not fit with the American way of taking charge and getting things done. For instance, we often plan the solutions before we embark on a short-term mission trip. We collect our luggage at a foreign airport and jump into projects without sufficiently involving and listening to the local people we are seeking to serve. Mission committees are typically sincere and compassionate, yet the results of their intentions are not always sound because they are based on insufficient information. If we don't understand the problem, how can we choose an appropriate solution? What looks like a good plan in the church boardroom may not seem as wise on the steep streets of a Peruvian village.

A key initial step in understanding a problem is gaining perspective about the local environment and social conditions. A good doctor will first ask probing questions about a patient's family history, health, dietary habits, and personal relationships before making a diagnosis. Similarly, we must approach missions opportunities with a spirit of inquiry. We risk proposing ill-fitting and ill-received solutions if we do not first humble ourselves to learn about the local culture and respect the local people.

A Christian author, well known for his bestselling book on praying for prosperity, made just such a mistake. After selling millions of copies of his book on prospering through prayer, Bruce Wilkinson moved his family to South Africa and launched a nonprofit organization to help Africans suffering from HIV/AIDS. The centerpiece of his efforts was to have been a grand theme park in Swaziland — including a golf course, cannery, chicken farm, schools, and churches, among other things — that would cater to Western tourists and house ten thousand AIDS orphans. Despite cautions from the U.S. ambassador, who warned Wilkinson that uprooting orphans from their communities went against Swazi culture, Wilkinson forged ahead. He gave the Swazi king five days to approve a plan that would give his nonprofit organization a ninety-nine-year lease on prime game parks, forcing out local environmental groups that had controlled the parks for decades.[4]

When the Swazi press caught wind of Wilkinson's proposal, they detected a scent of colonialism. Justified or not, the Swazi media turned popular opinion against the project. When he failed to get the king's approval for the tracts of land, Wilkinson quit the project and returned to the U.S., explaining that Swazi traditions had failed to adequately provide for the multitudes of poor AIDS orphans, and that drastic new measures and bold dreams were required. Wilkinson's heart may have been in the right place, but how would things have turned out if he had adequately engaged the locals and listened to their ideas before proposing his solutions?

CONFUSING RELIEF WITH DEVELOPMENT

A helpful first step in thinking about working with the poor in any context is to discern whether the situation calls for relief, development, or some combination of the two. Relief is a rapid provision of temporary resources to reduce immediate suffering. When we see need, we think of providing relief. James 2:16 questions, "If one of you says to [the man with physical needs], 'Go, I wish you well; keep warm and well fed,' but does nothing about his physical needs, what good is it?"

I found myself in this situation recently in Haiti. We were visiting a small village and saw a small child with sores on his body and fluid coming out of his ears. When we asked the mother if she had visited the hospital, she responded, "Yes, but I just didn't have the funds required for the prescription." Looking at her other children, her house, and her surroundings, we knew she was telling the truth. This woman was clearly among the poorest of the poor. What must it be like to know how to heal your child but to have no way of coming up with a modest amount of money for critical medicine? We knew that the urgency of this situation required an immediate response. The knowledge that we were engaged in bringing longer-term sustainable economic development to her community did nothing for the immediate need of her sick child. We secretly gave the necessary money to a local staff member and asked him to ensure that this child received proper treatment.

Despite occasions like this when short-term immediate aid is required, we know that longer-term development is a preferable response. Certainly it would be better if this mother had an income sufficient to guarantee that if her kids fall sick she will be able to pay for their treatment. Giles Bolton, a veteran African diplomat, describes the difference between relief and development: "In consumer language, [development] is a bit like making an investment rather than an immediate purchase ... [It's a] much better value if it works because it gives poor people control over their own lives

and enables them better to withstand future humanitarian disasters without outside help."[5]

Both relief and development can be appropriate interventions, but if we *sustain* relief efforts instead of transitioning to longer-term development, we hurt the very people we are trying to help.

UNINTENDED CONSEQUENCES

After the 1994 genocide in Rwanda, many Christian organizations were motivated to rebuild this broken country. Following the example and admonitions of Jesus to feed the hungry, clothe the naked, and show compassion to the hurting, these organizations and their dedicated people responded. Churches in America rebuilt Rwandan churches and schools, sent food aid and supplies, and attempted to address the unimaginable physical and psychological damage inflicted by the hundred days of terror. Several years after the genocide, peace and stability allowed Rwanda to transition from a country needing emergency assistance to one needing long-term development. Unfortunately, many churches and aid organizations failed to recognize this, leading to frustrations like that encountered by a Rwandan named Jean.

After the genocide, Jean seized an opportunity to begin a small poultry business to provide his neighborhood with eggs. He managed to scrape together funds to purchase several fowl, and his business grew. Later, a church in America "adopted" the village where Jean lived and worked. The church decided to donate clothes and supplies. They also imported eggs from a neighboring community and gave them away. Suddenly, this one village was flooded with surplus eggs. It is not difficult to imagine what happened to Jean's business: people went first to collect the free eggs and bought Jean's eggs only when the supply of free eggs was depleted. The market price for eggs plummeted in Jean's village and, as a result, Jean was forced to sell his productive assets, his chickens.

The next year, after Jean had left the poultry business, the church that had supplied the free eggs turned its attention to another disaster in another part of the world. Jean's community had no capacity to produce eggs locally and was forced to import eggs from a neighboring town. The cost of these eggs was higher than the eggs Jean had sold, so both Jean and his village were hurt economically by the good intentions of one American church.

Have you ever donated your used T-shirts to your local thrift store? Often these are bundled and shipped to Africa. This business of second-hand Western clothing, called the *mivumba* trade in East Africa, decimated clothing production in countries like Uganda and Zambia that previously had thriving textile industries. Several other countries, including Nigeria and Eritrea, have imposed significant tariffs on foreign imports to avoid a similar fate.[6] It is hard to comprehend that our used T-shirts could harm local producers on another continent, yet the American church must learn to be aware of such consequences in our increasingly interconnected world.

FOCUS ON THE FOREIGNERS

If we were to hold an impartial mirror to our hearts, we would have to admit that sometimes our "noble" actions are self-serving. We in the West who have been so blessed with material wealth often feel guilty about our relative prosperity and good fortune compared with our distant brothers and sisters in the developing world. Guilt can motivate us to "bless others as we have been blessed." And yet we face a serious problem if we act out of a desire for clear consciences that enable us to continue living in abundance.

I hosted a group of church members who traveled to Rwanda to visit HIV/AIDS, maternal health, and economic development programs that they had been supporting for several years. As we drove around the hilly countryside, they tossed handfuls of candy out the window at random groups of Rwandans they passed. They were filled with happiness at the thought that they were bringing joy to this country and making a difference. The local staff members were embarrassed, but they kept silent because they did not want to offend their guests. These local staff members knew long-term actions like this transform some poor but hardworking Rwandans into beggars and exacerbate the poor dental health of the region.

CONNECTING HEADS AND HEARTS

After hearing about the unintended consequences of very good intentions and reflecting on our own culpability, it might be easy to slip toward hopelessness and discouragement. "We're just trying to help!" a friend complained after seeing a missions project fail. "I didn't know it was going to be so hard … I feel like giving up." Something in us knows that it isn't right to turn a blind eye to the enormous needs in our world — that doesn't square with the biblical teaching on compassion and action. But just as inaction is not an option for followers of Christ, neither should we act inappropriately. We want to do more than just care about the poor — we want to find solutions that make a permanent difference.

We are required to do the hard work of continually evaluating our actions and determining what is most helpful to the people we're seeking to serve.

It is necessary to connect heads and hearts and to fully engage both for God's glory. There is a problem if we have one without the other. Our desire is to see the church move from well-intentioned blunders to thoughtful, compassionate acts of mercy that result in lasting change.

WHERE NOW?

If there were easy ways to alleviate poverty, we would have found them by now. Collectively, the world has spent $2.4 trillion of government aid on international development programs. Finally we're beginning to wonder: Where are the results? The Hudson Institute estimates religious organizations give a little over $4 billion per year to international causes, and it is time for the church to ask the same question. After all of the good intentions, where are the results? Have our good intentions truly made an impact on poverty and expanded Christ's kingdom around the world?

If funding were all that was required, many more of the world's problems would be solved by now. Increased funding will neither end global poverty nor fulfill the church's mandate. There is a growing consensus that different approaches and tools are needed for the church to effectively care for the spiritual and physical needs of the poor.

Thankfully, successful models of a new approach to serving the poor are emerging. I think of a dim room at the house of a loan client from Urwego, a microfinance institution in Rwanda. She was poor by the world's standards, but she instructed her daughter to run out to buy me a cold Coke. As a client of Urwego, she had borrowed money to grow her business of making embroidered furniture covers. Now that she was enjoying some modest success, she was eager to be a gracious hostess to her guest from America. She proudly directed my attention to the new tin panels on her roof. "For the first time in my life, my family and I don't get wet during the rainy season!" she proclaimed. Mama Ndugu derived joy from using her skills to provide for herself and her family. She described how her relationship with her loan officer had changed the way she looked at the church. She saw the church as a place of healing and service, and her loan officer was showing her a very different picture of what a follower of Jesus acts like.

What separates examples like Mama Ndugu from the pitfalls previously described? One of the main differences is that employment produces dignity and creates a sustainable solution to poverty.

4

A HAND UP, NOT A HANDOUT

(PETER)

Marcel, a thirty-year-old friend from Rwanda, wrote an email stating, "I am not good because there has been a long time without a job. I am still looking for a job. My life is not going well for me." Marcel was not making a veiled plea for a handout; he truly wanted an opportunity to use his skills and abilities to provide for his needs. The more time we spend listening to the people we are trying to serve, the more we will hear Marcel's refrain repeated in various contexts and within various cultures — people living in poverty know that a handout is inferior to an opportunity to work and provide for one's own long-term needs. Nearly every human prefers the dignity that comes from employment to the demeaning dependence of handouts.

In the United States, we often have a skewed view of work. We might complain about our coworkers, the coffee, the cost of health care, and the lack of vacation. We might complain about our boss and the buzzing of the lights. With all this complaining, we might start to believe that our job is a curse.

Work is *not* a curse. God worked as he created the universe. Adam and Eve had plenty of work to do in caring for the Garden. All of this work occurred before sin entered the world. Properly understood, work is a blessing. If you don't believe me, ask someone in the developing world who doesn't have a job. That individual will be able to describe the harm that results from unemployment and how the absence of employment is a much more significant curse than whatever "cursed" job you might have.

A look at the example of ancient Israel and the history of the United States supports the assertion that employment is the best way to address long-term physical poverty.

BIBLICAL SUPPORT

Ancient Israel had a systematic code governing the care of the poor. Israel understood what it was like to be poor and oppressed as a result of their bondage in Egypt. Shortly after their miraculous exodus, God provided a system of laws that codified their care for the poor.

In the book of Ruth we see a successful businessman, Boaz, cultivating his fields but taking special care to leave some of the field for Ruth, a widow and foreigner from Moab. Boaz was following the requirement in Deuteronomy 24:19: "When you are harvesting in your field and you overlook a sheaf, do not go back to get it. Leave it for the alien, the fatherless and the widow, so that the Lord your God may bless you in all the work of your hands." This law was echoed in the ancient rabbinic tradition: "One who prevents the poor from gathering gleanings or allows one poor person to gather and prevents another from doing so, is deemed a robber of the poor."[1]

In addition to this specific command, other Old Testament laws governed the ability to reclaim lost land so that individuals could return to work, mandated that wages be paid promptly, and ensured that a high level of care was provided to employees. Notice that these specific laws were designed to protect employment opportunities, not facilitate endless handouts. For example, in "sharing the harvest," a widow or foreigner was required to do the gathering and the threshing. Work was still required.

In the New Testament, Paul warns the church in Thessalonica: "If a man will not work, he shall not eat" (2 Thessalonians 3:10) and sets the expectation that everyone capable of working should provide for themselves and their families. He recognized that giving aid to individuals who have the capacity to work could deprive resources from those who truly need them. Paul himself lived this principle as he sewed tents and labored so that he would not be a burden to supporting churches. To the Ephesians, Paul writes, "He who has been stealing must steal no longer, but must work, doing something useful with his own hands, that he may have something to share with those in need" (Ephesians 4:28). In this situation, employment is the tool that helps turn robbers into generous givers.

These are just a few examples of a broader theme woven throughout Scripture that the preferred system to care for the poor is one that uses God-given abilities in productive employment.

HISTORICAL EXAMPLES

The historical record of charity in the United States shows a model similarly focused on employment and responsibility instead of handouts.

At our nation's founding, it was considered immoral to give aid to those who had the capacity to work. This would be robbing resources from those who truly need them, thus harming the people the aid was meant to help. Cotton Mather, the influential Puritan minister, stated in 1698, "I will rather utter an exhortation ... that you may not abuse your charity by misapplying it."[2] Mather recognized that charity has the potential to do enormous good for people who need it, but that the greatest threat to charity could be those who indiscriminately give charity without appropriate engagement and involvement of the recipient.

At that point in our nation's history, when an individual asked for assistance, the first response was to look at the situation. If the individual had the ability to work, then the individual was given work. And there was certainly plenty to do in the "New World." Food-for-work programs began, and hostels for the needy almost always required some sort of contribution. The idea of someone "mooching" was intolerable, and aid was cautiously distributed only after the individual's situation was evaluated. Cotton Mather succinctly encouraged his congregation to find employment for the poor. "Find 'em work; set 'em to work; keep 'em to work."[3]

As America prospered, charity grew exponentially. The early 1900s saw a particularly high growth rate of charitable giving; between 1911 and 1925, sixteen of the largest cities increased their relief payments from $1.6 million to $14.7 million, a 918 percent increase.[4] With this growth came a professionalization and delocalization of charity as well as a slow shift away from employment-producing programs. When the Great Depression hit, President Franklin D. Roosevelt hoped that his New Deal responses would be only a temporary solution. In November 1933 he stated, "When any man or woman goes on a dole something happens to them mentally and the quicker they are taken off the dole the better it is for them the rest of their lives."[5] Many of the New Deal programs were designed not around entitlement but on employment. Charity was, and is, best seen as a temporary assistance to bridge the gap between need and employment.

Unfortunately, many American churches have slipped into a charity mind-set and do not follow the historical or the scriptural example. This shift away from employment has unintentionally crippled the church's long-term impact on poverty.

THE BENEFITS OF EMPLOYMENT OVER CHARITY

Do you remember how you felt when you received your first paycheck? In middle school I mowed elderly Mrs. Johnson's lawn. She would inspect my work and acknowledge that I had cut close enough to her barn and not missed any sections under her apple trees. Then she would invite me into her house, offer me a cold Tang mixed with her special spices, and pay me for my work. I enjoyed a strong sense of satisfaction as she expressed her pleasure with a job well done.

Relying on charity might provide enough for a bare existence, but it will never be enough to help a poor man off his knees. Charity will never allow an individual to be the way God created humankind to be — productive in caring for the earth and using the strength and skills he gave. And besides, charity isn't what the poor want.

We've all heard the saying, "If you give a man a fish, you feed him for a day, but if you teach a man to fish, you feed him for life." These well-worn words contain an important truth: Who would settle for an occasional fish dropped off on your doorstep if you had the opportunity to start your own fishing business?

Drawing on his personal experience with the Waodoni tribe, missionary Steve Saint writes, "We may be the wealthiest nation and the wealthiest Christians on earth, but that is not a good reason to give someone something." Saint goes on to describe the following challenges that come from long-term handouts:

- *No Value:* It is much more difficult to appreciate the value of something that costs us nothing. Consequently, it does not last as long.

- *Personal Devaluation:* If people are always given things, they begin to expect the things, thereby negating personal dreams or aspirations of climbing out of their current condition. Always being on the receiving end encourages indigenous believers to see themselves as incompetent, unable to learn even if they did decide they wanted to learn.

- *Desire Becomes Necessity:* Giving a gift to one person can result in everyone else wanting one as well. Similar but more critical is the possibility that if the first gift proves effective there will suddenly be a legitimate need for many more. And if you cannot give the same tool to everyone, it is better not to give it to anyone. Help make it affordable, and then everyone can buy their own.[6]

FLYING KITES

When we engage in employment-based solutions, the benefits of employment extend to future generations. Outside a small office in Trou Du Nord, Haiti, I saw several boys with homemade kites. Using a plastic bag, some string, and a few sticks, these three boys constructed kites capable of expertly navigating tangled power lines and two-story buildings. I could see other kids watching and learning from their example. Other children saw what was possible, and there grew a prestige factor in who could get his kite the highest.

In the same way, I've seen community members improve their lives,

and their hard work motivates other community members to action. If my neighbor can pull his family out of poverty, why can't I? Essentially, they are pushing the limits of what is possible, and from very little they are making kites that can fly higher and higher.

Employment decreases the need for never-ending support. There is an exit strategy for any external assistance provided. Many churches are beginning to recognize that their international assistance has built churches, trained pastors, fed the poor ... and somehow created a web of dependency from which there is no way out. They have not built the surrounding economic infrastructure to ensure the longevity of these worthy efforts.

Contrast this type of situation with Oleg Bulgaru's experience. After receiving two loans from Invest-Credit in Chisinau, Moldova, Oleg's furniture production and assembly business had become profitable enough to support both his family and his ministry. The loans enabled Oleg to remain in his apartment with his family despite rising rents, purchase sufficient food, and save for his daughter's education.

Oleg now uses his business profits to supply local prisoners with food, medicine, books, and clothing. Oleg and his four business partners are all former prisoners who now minister to this at-risk population in Chisinau. When prisoners are released, Oleg and his team buy them new clothes and shoes, help pay their first month's rent, and, most importantly, help them find jobs. Oleg is pleased that his business now fully supports this prison ministry. He hopes that his business will continue to expand so that he can begin similar ministries in other local prisons. This model is so much more lasting, relational, and appropriate than if you or I started a prison ministry in Chisinau.

WHERE TO BEGIN?

If gifts don't create long-term change, and handouts tend to keep people on their knees, and if the only lasting solution for the poor is through employment, does that let us off the hook? Absolutely not! We have the potential to play a critical role in advancing employment opportunities and helping the poor to dramatically improve their lives.

But how? What can you and I do that actually helps? First we need to understand what it would be like to be born in rural Siem Riep, Cambodia. Over a decade ago, I briefly worked in this town situated a day's boat ride north of the capital, Phnom Penh, and it provided my first glimpse into rural poverty. Every day after work, I would jump on a moped and speed away to watch the sunset from the pinnacles of the temples of Angkor Wat, the "Asian pyramids." On my drive there, I would pass farmers wading in rice fields, planting, and I would try to understand what life would be like if I were born into their situation.

In Cambodia, 75 percent of the population works in the agricultural sector, most working on a family farm at a subsistence level.[7] If you were born to a rural farm family and stopped your education at the fourth grade, how could you secure one of the competitive positions of formal employment? How would you even know about job openings? You wouldn't receive a newspaper. You wouldn't know about posting your "résumé" on Monster. com. If you weren't related to someone already inside an organization that offered formal employment or didn't have sufficient savings to bribe your way in, you wouldn't have a chance.

In many developing countries, if you did receive a job offer, you would be required to pay a "deposit." The practice of requiring deposits is one of the most oppressive systems for poor employees. Outside Pune, India, rural laborers are paid $.85 per day and yet are required to provide a deposit of up to $50 without any documentation or guarantee that these funds will be returned at the cessation of employment.

Consider the reality of life for the poor. What could you do to earn money beyond your meager wages from subsistence agriculture or day labor for an oppressive employer? Your only option would be to create your own employment. What would you do to provide a better life for your children? How would you start? What would you need?

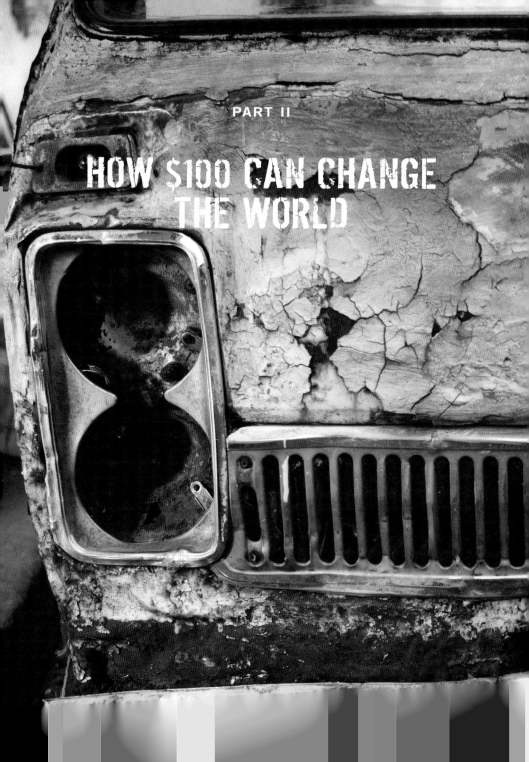

PART II

HOW $100 CAN CHANGE THE WORLD

5

UNLOCKING ENTREPRENEURSHIP

(PETER)

You don't have to be an economist to understand capital. Consider Abdul Saboor. Abdul runs a small television repair business in Kabul, Afghanistan. He received a small loan to increase his inventory of spare parts, to hire two additional people to help manage his growing business, significantly improving his efficiency. "I used to have to go to the market [by foot] every day to buy parts," he said, adding that it was a two-and-a-half-hour round trip. "Now I go once every two weeks."[1]

It's that simple. He used a loan to open a second shop, which increased his sales and thus his profits. More importantly, he increased his efficiency and productivity and provided jobs for two more people.

ECONOMIC STIMULUS

Access to capital can unlock the enterprising potential inherent within every individual. Capital empowers the poor, allowing them to improve their bargaining power and leverage, which can lead to lower costs, higher productivity, and an improved standard of living. According to Peruvian economist Hernando de Soto, "Capital is the force that raises the productivity of labor and creates the wealth of nations ... It is the foundation of progress and the one thing that poor countries cannot seem to produce themselves, no matter how eagerly their people engage in all the other activities that characterize a capitalist economy."[2]

Stated simply, it takes money to make money. The usual two ways to access that initial capital are through a savings account or a loan. If you ask individuals from virtually any culture who have succeeded in business, you will nearly always hear a story about their first loan that helped put them on the path to building a successful business.

The benefits of capital seem obvious enough to Americans — and we're usually able to acquire the capital we need. Banks, financing companies, and affluent relatives abound in the U.S. and in other developed countries. However, the four billion impoverished people in developing countries have absolutely no access to capital at a reasonable cost — often no access at any cost. How can the poor access modest amounts of capital with which to start and grow their businesses?

LOANS

Yesterday in the mail I received three offers from credit card companies. One touted double airline miles, another guaranteed zero-percent interest for all balance transfers for the life of the loan, and another boasted about the size of loan that I was prequalified to receive. None of the offers interested me, and I quickly threw them out. However, during my lunch break, I visited Home Depot and was approached by a woman wearing an orange apron covered with pins. Linda offered me $20 or 10 percent off my purchase if I signed on a dotted line and accepted a Home Depot credit card. Now *that* was an offer I couldn't refuse — $20 is enough money to pay a babysitter so I can have an evening out with my wife!

My ubiquitous access to easy and relatively affordable credit could not be further away from the reality of individuals living in Parola, Philippines. When we visited this high-crime area, the going rate for moneylenders was 20 percent. Not a bad interest rate — until we realized that this rate was for four days! Apparently the crime in this area did not just result from robbers and pickpockets; it also came through usurious interest rates on capital and individuals who preyed on those with no other options.

In many parts of the world, "5 – 6" loans are the norm. Individuals borrow five units and repay six, equaling a 20 percent interest rate. Again, the problem is that this rate is either daily, weekly, or monthly, depending on the particular loan shark. How would it be possible to escape a vicious loan cycle with rates this high? Consider a loan of $100, perhaps used to take a sick relative to the city for medical treatment. At 20 percent weekly interest, that $100 loan could quickly grow to a staggering $1,849 after just sixteen weeks. It would be an inescapable trap for all who fall into it.

Later we'll describe innovative ways that individuals and organizations use to access much more reasonably priced capital. But if rates for loans are so ridiculously high for many of the poor, perhaps savings is a better route for them to accumulate the modest amount of capital necessary to launch a business.

SAVINGS

There are many benefits to saving instead of taking a loan. Saving is less risky, more flexible, and accumulates money to invest in a business or provide for emergencies. So why don't the poor save? Our situation in the West differs markedly from the experience of the majority of the world. I remember opening my first savings account with my father at Middlesex Bank on Main Street in Concord, Massachusetts, and how I began saving small amounts. I put an advertisement in the local paper expressing my willingness to work hard and do any odd jobs. Within a week, I was flooded with opportunities to move pianos, paint sheds, haul rocks, and mow lawns. Each week I would tithe and put a portion in savings at Middlesex Bank. Slowly these savings grew, and I remember my excitement at having accumulated enough in my account to purchase my first Huffy mountain bike.

Contrast my experience to Geetha, who in seven months will need 1,000 Indian rupees — about $25, a lot of money in her situation — for school fees for her daughter. She only makes $28 a month, so if she doesn't start saving the money now, she'll never have such a large sum.[3]

No banks or similar services are available to Geetha. So, to get that amount, she agrees to save with Jyothi, her friendly neighborhood "Savings Collector." Jyothi has recognized Geetha's need for savings and has developed a business to meet that demand. Jyothi goes to Geetha and her other clients each day to collect savings deposits from them. In this way, Geetha saves 5 rupees a day. After doing this for 220 days, Geetha will have deposited 1,100 rupees, and she will then get back 1,000. Jyothi keeps 100 as her fee for providing this valuable service.

Geetha has saved the 1,000 rupees needed to pay her daughter's school fees — but by getting back less than she put in, she actually paid to save! How much has Geetha paid to save for the school fees for her daughter? She's paid 30 percent APR.[4] Can you imagine? We Americans *earn* money on our savings, while Geetha and others like her are forced to pay for the privilege. And many in the world do not even have access to a savings collector. This demonstrates how vital savings are to the poor.

Conducting a study to determine if HOPE International should expand its services to a rural fishing village on the Congo River, our group asked several locals a simple question: "If you only have a little money to save, what choices do you have?" Most said they have only one option — travel to the center of the next town and deposit their funds at a savings kiosk. And when they withdraw savings from the kiosk, they pay 10 percent of the maximum balance. One of the potential borrowers I met would be required to pay $.15 for transportation plus a 10 percent fee to save $1. If he wanted to save $1 a week for six months, he just paid $6.50, or 25 percent of his total savings, for the privilege. What an incredible negative savings rate!

My first reaction to hearing these exorbitant rates the poor pay to save was, "That's crazy! Why pay someone to collect and hold your savings for you? Why don't the poor just do it themselves, especially when this type of savings arrangement isn't even FDIC insured?" This is a common response to learning that poor people like Geetha often pay deposit collectors 30 percent APR in order to save in a place that is only marginally more secure.

The key to making sense of this is to recognize the enormous obstacles to saving in developing countries. These obstacles are related to the following:

- The reality of living conditions (no place to safely hide cash)
- The enormous social demands of communal societies
- The lack of alternatives

Reality of Living Conditions. If you lived in a five-by-eight-foot tin house with no doors or windows and practically no furniture, where would you hide your cash? How would you protect against theft? Natural disasters can literally burn, rot, or sweep away the cash savings that people have tried to squirrel away in hiding places in or near their homes. Mozambique's severe floods of 2000 provide an example. Following a prolonged period of torrential rain, a dam broke and flash floods swept into villages and towns in the middle of the night. In the darkness, people fled for their lives in great panic. They had no chance of first digging in the ground, now covered by several feet of water, for the buried bottles or tin cans in which they had tried to protect their money. In some cases, it took months for the floods to recede. When people returned to their villages, they found that their huts had literally been washed away. Nothing remained. Individuals who buried their cash in the ground or hid their savings under furniture didn't know where to look. Even those who hid their money near landmarks that withstood the flooding lost their savings; the money had decomposed from the moisture.

Societal Demands. In many developing countries, familial and communal ties are so strong that it would be social suicide to deny someone money if you have some to spare. Those who have even a little are expected to share with a brother, aunt, cousin, or neighbor who asks. Denying the request would lead to ostracism from the community. Although there are great benefits to a society that shares so completely, it holds people back from accumulating and investing capital — and thus moving forward economically. It is often a question of short-term gain at the cost of long-term progress — or money used for relief instead of development, as we discussed earlier.

Lack of Alternatives. In the United States, banks routinely try to attract our business. However, in the Democratic Republic of Congo, to cite one example, the banking situation is quite the opposite. Banks exist to serve the wealthy and have barriers that keep the poor from entering their premises. Minimum balance requirements and fees are the most formidable barriers. To open an account, many banks in the DRC require a minimum deposit of $300, about twice the average annual income in that area. By their policies and requirements, the formal banking infrastructure makes it abundantly clear that the poor are not welcome.

ALTERNATIVE PIGGY BANKS

So how *do* the poor save? Out of necessity, they have created a number of innovative options — though the options aren't ideal.

On a recent trip to Santiago, Dominican Republic, we met a woman who manufactures bamboo savings logs. She cuts twelve-inch lengths of naturally hollow bamboo stems, seals both ends, and then cuts small slits through which money can be deposited. She described how most customers bury them or hide them underneath a piece of furniture. When asked if they ever put them under their mattresses, she laughed and cautioned, *"Everyone* knows that's where people hide extra money, so you really shouldn't hide your money there."

Another creative savings method was discovered by a British nongovernmental organization operating in Cambodia. At one point, its leaders noticed that many Cambodians raise pigs, so they concluded that it must be a profitable business. Perhaps they could help even more Cambodians to take advantage of pig farming. However, after talking with several pig farmers and running the numbers, they were bewildered — the local farmers were *losing* money on their pigs! The cost of raising the pigs exceeded the income received when the pigs were sold. What was going on?

Further research revealed the truth: the Cambodian farmers were raising pigs as a way to save a "lump sum" of money that could be used for school fees, weddings, or to grow their business.

One Cambodian farmer explained it this way: "If I don't have a pig to raise, each day I'll fritter away whatever money I have, partly by responding to the requests of relatives and friends. In three months, I'll have nothing more than I do now. However, if I have a pig, I *have* to take care of it. I have to invest my daily loose change into the pig — I can't allow it to starve or get ill and die. After a few months of this, I'll sell it and use the money for my son's school fees."[5] This farmer was using a literal piggy bank that could protect his money from constantly diminishing in small ways.

This farmer's loss on his pig enterprise is similar to the savings fees paid by Geetha, the woman who "earned" a negative 30 percent on her savings. She paid that much to her deposit collector to enjoy the benefits of a future lump sum.

OTHER BENEFITS OF SAVINGS

It might seem counterintuitive, but individuals living in poverty are too poor *not* to save. There are few governmental safety nets in developing countries. Small emergencies can become disasters. Dave Larson, international development expert, describes savings this way:

The poor are like someone on the edge of a steep, tall cliff. Perilously near the edge, it won't take much of a blow to force them over the edge into a tragic fall. A fire, a flood, a drought, an illness, an accident — these and other traumas could easily result in catastrophe. Savings helps people reduce their vulnerability. In effect, it allows them to take a few steps away from the edge. Farther away, they are at less risk. A blow may push them toward the edge — but not over. When we help people to save money we're saving lives — in less dramatic but perhaps far more effective ways than we see in the movies. Rather than arriving in a helicopter to grab someone dangling from tree roots atop a cliff, we're helping them to stay away from the tree roots in the first place.

Mike Cahill, a home builder from Pennsylvania, traveled with HOPE International to the Dominican Republic in 2007 to visit Esperanza, a microfinance institution. In one small community outside San Pedro, Mike and the team visited Yaquelia, a woman who had just started benefiting from Esperanza's services. When Mike asked Yaquelia about her family, she told the group about her five-year-old son Juan, who was suffering from hydrocephalus. It was obvious that this was a severe medical need and that Juan needed to be treated. Upon returning to the United States, Mike did everything he could to get medical treatment for Juan and found a doctor willing to perform the surgery. Unfortunately, after medical examination, they determined that it was too late to treat this abnormality. The tragedy is that Juan could have been cured if his mother had sufficient savings and the knowledge of how to care properly for her son.

This tragic situation is repeated throughout the world. U2's Bono calls this sort of situation "stupid poverty" and wonders why thousands of individuals should die every day from mosquito bites, starvation, and preventable diseases.[6] There simply is no good reason why thirty thousand children should die each day from preventable diseases. Poverty is behind almost every one of those unnecessary deaths, and in countless cases, a small savings account could have prevented tragedy.

Ephraim Kabaija, former chief of staff to President Paul Kagame of Rwanda and currently the president's adviser on rural development, explained the critical need for a bank that offers savings accounts to the Rwandan people:

> Do you know how many children die in our country every year because their mothers cannot afford the $2 to $10 needed to buy medicines to treat diarrhea, fever, malaria, and other common illnesses? Do you appreciate how much angst, misery, and despair we could eliminate from our country if every family had $50 in a savings account?[7]

PREPARING FOR THE FUTURE

For many in the developing world, everything revolves around *today*. What will I eat today? What will I wear today? Where will I find employment today? Beginning to accumulate savings helps shift an individual's focus from today to tomorrow. A family's timeline begins to change. The emotional benefits of this are hard to quantify, but a street vendor in Congo summarized it best: "I'm not so afraid of tomorrow anymore."

The reality is that having a safe place to save small amounts of capital or access a loan is essential if people are to escape poverty and build a better future. But if the answer isn't national banks or deposit collectors or high-interest loans, what is it?

6

A BRASS RING
FOR THE POOR

(PHIL)

I treasure a photograph of my daughter on an antique carousel near the River Seine in Paris. In the background, the Eiffel Tower is an iron miracle looming in a peacock blue sky. Laura is twelve — still young enough to delight unselfconsciously in the lively music and bright colors. She is laughing as she talks my recently retired father into joining her on one of the bright red horses.

A century ago, the operators of these rotating machines would place a brass ring on an iron arm and swing it just out of reach of the outside row of children. If a child could somehow grasp the ring as they went by, they would get a prize. From that practice we get the phrase "grabbing the brass ring." Millions of poor people have grabbed their brass rings from a very different type of merry-go-round.

Poor families living in the developing world desperately need both secure ways to save money and access to affordable credit. These are essential needs, and people have long found innovative ways to save and borrow lump sums of cash, including the method to be discussed next. Don't be fooled, as I once was, by the simplicity of the method. For two years I dismissed it as unimportant, but I've come to believe it is one of the most powerful ways to help many poor people, especially if churches are involved.

I have learned that great power is found in simplicity — the simplicity of a merry-go-round. To illustrate this, consider the following fictional example of how friends and relatives join together to empower one another.

Anna and Bonita invite their best friends, Clara and Delores, to join them in forming a savings club. They agree to meet at Anna's house for the next four Saturday nights, and each will bring $1, which they will save from their incomes. Each week they will put a total of $4 in a separate jar, and at the end of four weeks they will each take home a jar with $4 in it. The plan works well. At the end of four weeks, each one has saved $4 from their income.

It doesn't take too long for the women to see that it is both insecure and wasteful to keep money hidden in jars, so they agree to rotate turns in taking the jars home as they are filled. After a drawing to determine turns, Anna takes home the first filled jar, Bonita the second, Clara the third, and Delores the fourth. Again, at the end of four weeks, each one has a jar with

$4 in it. The same ending, but something was dramatically different in the two cases because of the timing when they received their jars.

In the second case, Anna's jar essentially contained $1 saved from her income plus $3 of loans from the others. The $3 of loans was repaid over the next three weeks out of her income. Bonita's jar (week two) essentially contained $1 saved from her income, $1 of repayment from Anna, and $2 of loans from Clara and Delores. Clara's jar (week three) contained $1 saved from her income, $2 of repayments from Anna and Bonita, and a $1 loan from Delores. Since Delores was last, her jar contained $3 of repayments from the others plus $1 saved from her income.

By working together and trusting each other, the women found a way to provide themselves loans and a way to save. In reality, those winning early places in the draw receive special benefits of loans. The ones late in the draw have to take additional risk. Only commitment and social pressure cause the early recipients of the jars to continue putting in their $1 every week. In a later example, I will show you how the poor have found a way to reduce this risk.

When each woman receives her jar, she then has several options. She can continue to save the money by keeping it in the jar, she can invest the money in her business, or she can choose to spend the money on household needs. She will make those choices depending on her needs and opportunities. One thing she must do, however, is make sure she can finish making the remainder of her $1 payments. The risks of the four women were limited since the obligation lasted for only four weeks. The most risk any of them took was the $3 Delores loaned to the others in the first three weeks.

This type of club has another important benefit hidden from most independently minded Americans. In a typical developing country, each person has a clear responsibility to care for family members, friends, and neighbors. If a person is able to accumulate any money, that person has a corresponding obligation to give or loan that money to someone else in need. This makes it nearly impossible for poor people to acquire any savings. However, if a poor person is committed to give money to a group, they have a higher social responsibility to fulfill that commitment, which outweighs all but the most dire emergency.

These types of groups are most commonly known as RoSCAs (Rotating Savings and Credit Associations). Other names include community managed loan funds, community managed microfinance, and village savings and loan associations. Locally, they may have other names, such as *consorcios* or *tandas* in Latin America, merry-go-rounds in Africa (having local names like *tontines* or *njangis*), and self-help groups in many parts of India. For the purposes of this book, we will use the term Savings and Credit Association (SCA) to refer to any type of community group that uses this rotating method of saving and lending.

You can already see some advantages of SCAs over other lending and savings methods typically available to poor people. Although it may choose to do so, an SCA does not have to charge a fee to save like a savings collector does. Although it may choose to do so, an SCA does not have to charge its members any interest or fees like money lenders or banks do. And, unlike banks, there is no minimum deposit, so even the poorest of the poor can participate.

Variations on SCAs have been around for hundreds of years, sometimes even in mission work. William Carey, the cobbler missionary to India who is recognized as the "Father of Modern Missions," used SCAs in the late 1700s in India to empower women. Carey agreed with Solomon that unless individuals have the power to save, they risk forever being slaves to lenders (Proverbs 22:7).

Yet as useful as these small groups are, their power expands exponentially as more members are added and other tweaks are made, as we'll discuss in the following sections.

EXPANDING THE MODEL

Let's continue learning from Anna and her friends. Finding their savings club to be helpful, the four women invite forty-eight neighbors to join them. Again, they agree to draw numbers, and again the draw amazingly comes out in alphabetical order. Anna drew #1, Bonita drew #2, and the others drew until Zoca drew #52. At the end of one year, all of them have saved $52 since they had all made fifty-two $1 payments out of their incomes. However, Anna received the equivalent of a $51 loan, and all the others except Zoca got loans of decreasing amounts. As they receive their payments, the members could invest in their businesses, save, or meet personal needs. By trusting each other and meeting their obligations, the club members created immense value that they shared.

MORE VARIATIONS ON A THEME

A casual glance at Anna's second, larger SCA shows the members are in very unequal positions due to the luck of the draw. Anna got her funds first, so she received a large loan. Zoca received her funds last, so she didn't get any loan. In addition, Zoca took the greatest risk that all members might not pay throughout the cycle and suffered the most from inflation. Fortunately, these inequities can either be equalized or turned into extra value for the members to share.

One of the inequities is that participants receive different amounts of loans because of their position in the draw. Some SCAs solve this dilemma by bidding out the right to receive the next payment to the members who have not yet received their payments. The money received in the auctions is often shared equally by either all of the members or just the members who have not yet received their payments. This allows the people who need a loan the most at any given time to receive it, while those who need one the least can wait and not pay extra to get a loan until it is their turn. It is not uncommon for the offer for the first payment in a large SCA to be as much as 20 to 50 percent of the amount of the first payment.

The auction process not only eliminates the unequal benefit of receiving loans early but it more fairly shares the risk of repayment and the effects of inflation. Clearly, those who receive the payments early in the cycle are the most likely to quit making their payments. The two primary safeguards against this are loss of social standing and acquiring a bad reputation so they cannot join in future SCAs in the community. Although these are strong incentives to continue making weekly payments, they are not fail-safe. So the innovative poor have found a way to mitigate the risk of repayment. They've also found a solution to the perplexing problem of recruiting trustworthy members. Finding reliable members and ensuring that everyone makes timely payments is quite a task. Having the time and contacts to find enough reliable members for large SCAs is difficult for a working poor person.

FOUNDERS

In very large SCAs, both repayment and organizational issues can be solved by having a founding member who is responsible for organizing the group, collecting payments, and guaranteeing timely payments. Additionally, a founding member makes it possible for the members to be strangers who don't necessarily live or work in the same location. Equally important, the founder can serve as a community liaison who educates people about the benefits of joining an SCA.

Founders obviously have costs involved with forming and running SCAs. So they may charge fees for their service, which vary in amount according to the time and risk involved. A typical founder fee might be to receive the first payment while not putting in any weekly payments. Under this type of fee structure, the cost of a founder is not justified until the size of the SCA is fairly large. For instance, if the SCA only had four other members, the cost of the founder's fee is about 20 percent, while with fifty other members it is less than 2 percent.

Some types of founders might be able to form groups for small fees. For example, assume a local grocer is the founding member of a small SCA. Her collecting costs — in terms of time and energy — would be minimal because members come to her store regularly anyway. She knows the creditworthiness of her neighbors and customers, and she has the power to withhold groceries until all payments are made. Since an SCA is a benefit to her community, and consequently to her, the grocer might be willing to form the SCA for a small cash fee. As we will discuss later, missionaries, churches, and charities might similarly choose to be founders for reasons other than making a cash fee.

In contrast, assume the founding member is a professional organizer who puts together large SCAs made up of people living in many locations. This is the business of the professional organizer, who has high costs and risks. A professional organizer might charge a high fee, but if it is spread out over many members, the percentage cost could be acceptable. The profit potential for organizing large SCAs is substantial. A few years ago I was approached to join a group of investors wanting to raise millions of dollars to form a large business that would act as a founding member for thousands of SCAs.

Founders and members must tailor the fee structure to fit each situation. Members of an SCA are typically willing to pay reasonable fees for the valuable services they receive.

RICKSHAW RoSCAs

Perhaps the best book written on SCAs is *The Poor and Their Money* by Stuart Rutherford. Unfortunately, the book is out of print. Rutherford tells this story of one of his favorite variations of SCAs:

Poor men driven from villages by poverty come to Dhaka where the only work they can get is to hire a rickshaw, for say 25 taka a day (about $0.63) and hope to earn a daily profit of, say, 80 taka (about $2). In the 1980s such men — illiterate and new to the city, and without any help from NGOs or other sources — devised a standard RoSCA system which has worked to the advantage of many thousands of them. Groups of them get together and agree to contribute 25 taka a day to a kitty which is held, for the time being, by a trusted outsider (often the keeper of the stall where they take their tea at the day's end). Every ten days or so there is enough in the kitty to buy one new rickshaw, and that rickshaw is distributed by lottery to one of the members. The process continues until everyone has his own rickshaw. They have learnt how to adjust the number of members, the daily contribution, and the interval between rounds, to best suit their cash-flow and the price of a rickshaw. But one of the finest innovations is the rule that once a member has "won" his rickshaw in a draw, he must from then on contribute *double* each day.[1]

Over time and in other countries, the amounts of money change and variations on the SCA are different. However, in all cases SCAs offer the poor a method to use their money to generate new opportunities to earn and save.

THE SKY IS THE LIMIT

The basic operations of SCAs are fairly simple, and they have multiple advantages and few disadvantages. As we have seen, with their immense creativity the poor have found ways to mitigate most of the disadvantages. One disadvantage is the inflexibility that each SCA member has to make the same payment every week for the same number of weeks even though individual opportunities and needs may vary greatly. There are two well-known solutions to this dilemma.

One simple way around this is for people to join more than one SCA. For instance, a woman might join one SCA that ends at the time school fees are due, another ending near the time when she needs to buy seed for planting, and a third providing her with $10 at the end of every month. One of my acquaintances told me that his mother lives in Belize and is continually a member of at least five SCAs.

Another solution is to modify the SCA so it works more like the credit unions so popular in the United States. Introducing the concept of record keeping allows members to pool their savings and make loans to themselves in variable amounts. Since there are no overhead costs, the pool of savings grows quickly as the borrowers are charged fees and interest. Limits on the size of the loans, terms of repayment, and amounts of interest and fees are set by the members or their elected leaders. It is in everybody's self-interest to make the terms such that there is a balance between the loans desired and the savings available. If the agreement is for the organization to exist for a long time, the members might regularly distribute the interest payments to themselves as dividends. If the agreement is for the organization to exist for a short time, the members might split the total pool equally among themselves on the last day. In either case, this arrangement is more able to meet the variable needs of both savers and borrowers than a simple SCA, but it is more complicated to run.

I once met with the representatives of a Russian cooperative who ran an organization like this. They paid their members a 25 percent annual interest rate on savings but charged their members 40 percent for loans. At those two rates, they were able to entice members to save but were still able to loan out all the money they wanted.

FINALLY, A SOLUTION FOR RURAL AREAS

Although SCAs work well in urban areas, a special advantage of SCAs is their ability to aid the rural poor in areas of low population density. Poor people in outlying areas are almost completely without access to formal financial services because it is often cost prohibitive for banks and large organizations to reach so far outside high-density urban and suburban centers. Since there is little room in rural SCAs for businesses to make big profits, it is up to government organizations and nonprofit organizations to find a way to share the idea if it is to have a major impact on the world.

One major advocate of church-centered SCAs is the Chalmers Center for Economic Development at Covenant College in Georgia. During 2005 – 2007, the Chalmers Center conducted a series of weeklong Christian Economic Development Institutes (CEDIs) in Uganda and Kenya. Hundreds of church leaders from dozens of countries were trained to promote SCAs in their churches and communities. God has used these CEDIs to impact the ministries of Anglican churches in East Africa in important ways:

1. The Anglican Church of Kenya has launched a Microenterprise Development Network, a training and equipping initiative that seeks to use SCAs and other forms of microfinance to minister to the spiritual and economic needs of the poor.

2. The Anglican Church of Uganda has passed a resolution stating its intent to help bring SCAs to every congregation in Uganda.

3. The Anglican Church of Rwanda has responded by inviting Hope International to help spread SCAs across the country.

Only time will tell what fruit will eventually come out of these initiatives, but the potential is enormous, as the combined membership of the Anglican churches of these countries is over thirteen million people.[2] We will further discuss this initiative and its early results in chapter 11.

In India, at least three million self-help groups have been trained by thousands of nonprofit organizations and government agencies since the late 1980s. Among US-based institutions, CARE, Catholic Relief Services, Pact, and Oxfam America have embraced this approach and have launched locally adapted versions of the model in many countries.[3] Some SCAs in Latin America have grown so large that they can lend people money to buy cars and houses. In a taxicab in New York City, I learned that SCAs are active in the United States. My driver said he thought at least half of all cab drivers participate in a similar model.

SCAs are an effective way for poor people to grab brass rings by empowering themselves to save money and obtain loans. While SCAs are simple to administer and nearly always without large fees to outsiders, they do lack the flexibility to meet certain needs exceeding an SCA's limits. To address these problems — and to bring even more essential financial services to the poor — a Bangladeshi economics professor pioneered a different type of microfinance.

7

MICROFINANCE
GOES MAINSTREAM

(PHIL)

On December 10, 2006, Muhammad Yunus was awarded the Nobel Peace Prize for his historic work with microfinance. When his name as winner was announced in October 2006, millions of people around the world had the same reaction: "Who is this guy, and what is microfinance?"

Yunus was the dean of the economics department at Chittagong University in Bangladesh. Unlike some of his academic peers, he never lost his compassion for the poor. Passing a poor neighborhood every day on his way to work, he began thinking of creative ways he could help unlock the entrepreneurial spirit and enterprising potential of the people he saw. He began to roam through villages, asking poor people about their sources of income and access to credit. What he learned was daunting — without access to loans at traditional banks (both for economic and geographic reasons), the poor were often trapped in harsh repayment cycles with local loan sharks who charged as much as 20 percent interest per day.

Rather than make the common assumption that poor people will not willingly repay loans, Yunus began thinking of a creative way for them to receive loans so they could prove themselves to be safe credit recipients. Rather than assume that administrative costs for managing countless small loans would be prohibitively expensive, Yunus visualized ways to reduce costs to a minimum. Instead of being defeated by the poor's lack of collateral or legal standing, he worked on a loan design that would overcome those problems. In the end, he had to answer a single basic question: "How can I make sure that the poorest of the poor will pay me back?"

To test his theories, Yunus decided more than three decades ago to personally invest $27 in small loans to help a group of poor women break free from loan sharks and increase their incomes by improving their small businesses. Unlike his peers, Yunus was not surprised when all the women repaid their loans. These loans were the beginning of Grameen Bank, a Bangladeshi institution that has now loaned nearly $7 billion and is 94 per-

cent owned by its borrowers.

Yunus's economic theories are the basis for modern microfinance. He continues to be an outspoken advocate of microfinance and is perhaps the most influential individual in international development. It is not an overstatement to say that he and other microfinance pioneers changed the trajectory of global economic development.

Thomas Edison said, "Genius is one percent inspiration and ninety-nine percent perspiration." The inspiration of Yunus and other microfinance pioneers was finding a way to collect loans made to poor people without collateral. The perspiration came from raising money and experimenting with different loan techniques until their ideas were proven correct. As a result of their genius, hundreds of millions of people have already benefited.

MICROFINANCE

Microfinance is defined as providing financial services, such as small loans, to poor people so they can increase their income and decrease their vulnerability to unforeseen circumstances. Microfinance has been successful around the world. It works for one simple and indisputable reason — the vast majority of the poor are willing and able to lift themselves from poverty if given an opportunity.

Musadidi took advantage of his opportunity. He had a small "pharmacy" on the outskirts of Lubumbashi, Democratic Republic of the Congo. When he opened his store, he bought medicines from a larger pharmacy far from his neighborhood. He would buy about $3 worth of medicine and take it back to his store. As soon as it was sold, he would close his store and send a child running to the larger pharmacy to buy more stock. When the child returned, Musadidi re-opened his store. This would happen several times a day, every day, because Musadidi could never buy more than a few dollars' worth of inventory at once. After receiving a $55 microloan, he was able to take public transportation into the center of town once a week and buy medicines in bulk, reducing his costs and increasing his stock. After two years of growing his business and paying back his loans, Musadidi saved $2,000 and was building a house for his family.

WHY IT WORKS

The vast majority of poor people in developing countries make their living through owning small businesses that run on a cash basis. Imagine running such a small business. All your transactions are cash, and you barely have enough money to pay the bills at the end of each day. You must pay the highest prices for your inventory and equipment because you can buy only in small quantities from a limited number of sellers. Your customers have access to only a small amount of inventory, which you have to sell at low prices because you are so desperate to make sales that you cannot refuse any reasonable offer. Your perishable goods decay quickly because you lack the equipment or space to preserve them. You travel to suppliers frequently, limiting the time you can spend at your business and adding significant travel costs. At the end of every day, you take your money and inventory home where you have no safe place to protect it from theft or the fires and water damage to which flimsy shelters are so susceptible. This is the reality of most small business owners in the developing world; it is untenable from a financial perspective. These poor business owners are always clinging to the edge of the cliff.

With small loans, however, poor entrepreneurs have found they can permanently improve their businesses and increase their incomes. They can buy in bulk, travel less frequently to buy inventory, stock more goods, offer services needed in their communities, and buy equipment needed to reduce labor costs and increase output. None of these basic business strategies are difficult to understand or execute if capital is available, but they are impossible otherwise.

WHO MAKES THE LOANS?

Microfinance institutions (MFIs) provide access to loans using capital from outside sources such as donors or commercial lenders. Until the late 1990s, most MFIs were nonprofit organizations that raised contributions through donors and used these contributions to make loans. By 2008, there were thousands of MFIs, many of which were operated as for-profit organizations. MFIs range in size from tiny organizations with a few thousand dollars making loans in a single community to huge organizations with hundreds of millions of dollars making loans in many countries.

The only contact many poor people ever have with an MFI is through a loan officer. Unlike American banks, where loan officers sit behind desks and award loans to the best applicants, MFI loan officers typically travel by foot, bike, or motorcycle to villages where they meet people, organize borrower groups, and make and collect loans.

As one review of MFIs observed, "The loan officer makes or breaks borrowers' experiences. In addition to being the face of the MFI, the loan officer can give clients the information and support they need to thrive in business and at home. During early discussions of the loan process, the loan officer can help determine the appropriate loan amount and how the client will earn enough to repay."[1]

We will go into greater detail about MFIs and loan officers, but first let's look at the types of loans they make and collect.

ABOUT THE LOANS

The sizes of microloans vary from country to country and from MFI to MFI, but the first loan made to a person is generally between one-quarter and one-third of their country's average annual income. In very poor countries, a first loan might be $50, while in more developed countries it might be $1,000. If the borrower pays back a loan on time, she typically qualifies for a follow-up loan of a bigger size.

A routine term for a microloan is six months with payments made weekly. For instance, a $100 loan might have weekly payments of $4 to $5. As the MFI collects these payments, it recoups money it can use to make new loans. With six-month loans, an MFI can easily recycle money twice in one year. However, because payments are made weekly, it is theoretically possible for an MFI to recycle money up to four times a year, every year. This is a distinct advantage of microfinance over typical charities that use money only once.

Like many people, when I first learned about microfinance, I assumed repayment rates would be poor. Surely many poor people would simply fail to live up to their end of the bargain, either because of circumstances, greed, or laziness. However, I was stunned to learn that the repayment rate of most well-run MFIs is greater than 95 percent and often tops 98 percent. For instance, Grameen Bank's repayment rate currently runs in excess of 98 percent. Although this statistic sounds outlandishly high to Americans (whose repayment rate on credit card debt in the fall of 2008 was dropping toward 90 percent), this is actually a rather typical repayment rate for MFIs around the world.

How did MFIs solve one of the most intractable problems of any lender — making certain people pay back their loans?

Dr. Yunus and other microfinance pioneers understood poor people lack collateral to secure their loans; therefore, any loans would have to be unsecured "signature" loans that are typically very risky. The solution to this problem was found in the concept of a social guarantee. Microfinance pioneers formed borrower groups of between six and eight women. Each woman received her own loan, but each member of the group cross guaranteed the loans of all the other group members. In other words, if a woman does not make a payment for her loan, the other members of her group have to make it for her. These cross guarantees are the primary reason most efficient MFIs have high repayment rates. Borrowers know it is in their best interest to support and discipline each other at business and at home. This system of accountability and support helps build strong borrowing groups and communities that have a common goal: to lift their families and communities out of poverty.

Enforcement of the cross guarantee is best for everybody in the long term. I once sat in a meeting where one of the borrowers did not show up to make her payment. The loan officer refused to end the meeting until the payment was made. Eventually one of the women left the partially covered shack to find the absent borrower and bring her to the meeting, where she made her payment. I assure you that the other borrowers were unhappy about wasting an hour of their time in the hot sun and they let her know it.

Another reason for high repayment rates is that borrowers who repay on time qualify for larger follow-up loans with which they can continue to grow their businesses and profits. This is a strong incentive to repay on time. Each borrower understands that the opportunity to access affordable capital is not one they can afford to squander. There is power in a mother who wants to provide for her family. If this is her one opportunity to expand her business and provide school fees and better nutrition for her family, she will move heaven and earth to repay her loan on time.

Since borrowers cross guarantee loans, most MFIs require weekly meetings so that payments are made in front of the entire group and so additional training can be offered. In later chapters we'll discuss how these regular meetings are another way in which borrowers can build their communities and receive other important benefits.

WHAT ARE THE INTEREST RATES?

After fees are included, the average annual interest rates on microfinance loans typically range between 30 and 50 percent. To put it in different terms, I typically think of the annual interest rates as being between 10 and 25 percent plus the rate of inflation for the country involved. Although these rates seem high, they are similar to the rates charged for unsecured signature loans in America. However, since the rates initially seem outlandishly high to most people, and since high interest rates are the primary source of criticism of microfinance, let's delve more into the reasons behind them.

A base assumption of microfinance is that an MFI should become self-sufficient so it can survive and service its customers for the long term. Although experts have different terms for levels of self-sufficiency, a self-sustaining MFI would have enough interest income to pay for inflation, defaults, and operational overhead. If the MFI does not have enough interest income to cover these costs, it has to raise more money, take money out of its loan base, or reduce its services.

Inflation is often the hardest factor to consider. It's not an obvious expense that shows up on the income statement or balance sheet. However, if its loan base is not increasing by the rate of inflation, the MFI is going backwards. One statistic that can be misleading is the inflation rates of different countries as given by various government agencies. Bluntly, many governments, especially in developing countries, publish inaccurate statistics. I recently met with some wealthy borrowers living in Russia who were able to borrow money from a state-controlled bank at 10 percent per year because the government wanted to have an interest rate policy consistent with a low inflation rate. These borrowers took the money back to their community where they deposited it as savings in a locally owned credit union for a rate of 25 percent per year. The citizens knew the true inflation rate was much higher than the government pretended and profited by acting in accordance with reality.

As mentioned earlier, loan defaults are generally low in MFIs, but even so, the income from interest must cover the defaults or the MFI's capital base is reduced.

Operational overhead includes the cost of loan officers, back office people, computers, travel, and other direct costs in the field. Even though these costs in many countries are low compared to America, they are still high when compared to the size of most MFI loan portfolios. Although tiny loans are involved, the entire loan process must be run with high operational precision. If the payment is only $1, it must be recorded the same as if it were a $100,000 payment. Another reason for high operational costs is that most MFIs provide other services — such as training and insurance — that are built into the cost of the loan. Furthermore, since loan officers travel to the clients, the clients don't need to spend the time and money traveling to cities where loans might be available. The travel costs of loan officers who trek to distant towns and villages are reimbursed indirectly through high interest rates.

Borrowers are typically much more concerned about having access to loans than they are about high interest rates. In most cases they have no other access to loans, and if they do, the interest rates from their other options are higher than from microfinance companies.

The MFI loan interest rate is not the crucial component in success or failure. Consider the woman who borrows $50 and pays it off weekly over six months. Even at an average interest rate of 50 percent per year, she only pays a little more than $6 in interest ($50 x 50 percent interest x ¼ year average outstanding). If she wisely invests the $50 in her business, she very likely will make far more than that in net income.

It is crucial for an MFI to charge interest rates that allow it to become self-sustaining in the long term so that it can continue to service its community. A financially solvent MFI means the community can count on having access to loans and other financial services.

INTEREST RATES ARE ONLY PART OF THE STORY

Many people living in the developed world do not understand that interest rates are not the whole story when it comes to the real cost of a loan. When I want a loan, I put in an application by Internet or by going to a local bank a couple of miles away. After a short wait, I either get the loan or I don't, depending on my credit rating. The time and cost of getting a loan are minimal. It's not that way for poor people in developing countries.

I once saw a confidential government report on farm loans in an Asian country. The report explained how poor people chose among their three

borrowing options: local money lenders at rates far exceeding 100 percent per year, government-sponsored MFIs with far lower interest rates, or government agencies that might not charge any interest at all. The farmers took into account many factors other than the interest rates, such as how far they had to travel to make the loan request, the cost of traveling, the time required to get loan approval, the likelihood of getting loan approval, the cost of bribes, and if another loan might be needed in the future. The report concluded that after all the relevant cost factors were taken into account, the farmers were correct to make use of all three loan options, depending on the specific circumstances at the time. These farmers understood there are many costs and considerations when choosing which loan option best suited their needs.

MICROFINANCE AND WOMEN

The vast majority of microloans — maybe 80 percent worldwide — are made to women. Men are more likely to be employed if there are jobs in the area, while women are more likely to run small household businesses. Men are more likely to be conscripted for the military and more likely to spend family money on drinking or other income-negative activities. Women are typically more reliable in repaying loans, as they tend to shoulder the burden of family support more than men. A Rwandan proverb states, "A woman is the heart of the home." Helping a woman helps her entire household. As microfinance specialist Robert Hickson notes:

> Women are more likely to use services in a way which will promote family well-being. They are more reliable borrowers in that they tend to return anything they have borrowed and are less likely to try to cheat. They tend to be more careful with the resources they have, using money more wisely, and are more likely to save. Moreover, they are generally supportive creatures, especially in a group, which is good for the overall morale of the poor to lift themselves out of poverty.[2]

Dorothy Njobvu Kanjautso is a thirty-four-year-old widow from an impoverished village outside of Lilongwe, the capital of Malawi. When Dorothy's husband died, she was unable to provide for her three children. In 2002, she received her first loan of $133 and used the money to build the Ketava Nursery and primary school to serve very poor children from her village. Dorothy opened the school's doors to ten children. With subsequent loans, Dorothy was able to hire teachers and increase her classroom space. Today, Dorothy employs seven teachers, and the school's two hundred students learn in four classrooms. Not only does Dorothy educate ten orphans for free and provide for her own three children, but she cares for three AIDS orphans and supports her mother.[3]

RESPONSIBLE USE OF CREDIT

One of the most important functions of an MFI is to educate its borrowers and potential borrowers about the responsible use of credit. In most cases, MFIs require their borrowers to use loans for a single purpose — to increase their incomes.

If borrowers cannot increase their income, it is unlikely they will be able to repay their loans, which is bad for everyone. MFIs take precautions to ensure that borrowers are not using their loans to repay other loans or to purchase consumer goods. They also don't allow spouses or other relatives to confiscate the loan. To maximize the impact of credit, the majority of the loan *must* be used to increase income.

DOES MICROFINANCE WORK?

This is the crucial question: Do the benefits of MFI loans justify the risks of borrowing? A growing number of studies demonstrate that microfinance loans increase income, diversify income and assets, and decrease the vulnerability of poor families. For example:

- Clients of BRI (Bank Rakyat Indonesia) reported an average client income increase of 112 percent.

- Clients of several MFIs in Ghana realized income increases of $36 (versus $18 for non-clients).

- The incomes of two-thirds of CRECER (Crédito con Educación Rural) clients in Bolivia increased, and clients reported income smoothing so they had regular access to food, clothing, and other household needs. Eighty-six percent of clients reported increased savings.

- Long-term (four years or more) BRAC clients in Bangladesh increased their household spending by 28 percent and assets by 112 percent. These clients also reduced vulnerability through income smoothing and asset increases.[4] Income smoothing is crucial when credit is not available. For instance, it may take $5 every day to feed your family, but if your money comes in at odd times, your family might starve while you are waiting to make a big sale.

There have been a limited number of impact assessment studies about microfinance, but the most powerful way of understanding the impact of microfinance is to see it in action. I became a microfinance believer when I walked by a bus stop in a small town in Ukraine.

I watched the bus unload only a few people, but an immense number of boxes. I turned to my microfinance loan officer "guide" and asked about the situation. He said, "The people getting off the bus are mostly our clients. They previously took small amounts of money to the neighboring city, bought a few goods, and came back to sell them that day. Depending on how much they sold, they went back the next day for replacement inventory. Now that they have more money from loans, they only go once a week, have more time to sell their goods, buy in bulk at reduced prices, and even buy goods to resell to other vendors. They have reduced transportation costs, pay less for their inventory, have a better selection of inventory, and even make money off the other vendors."

It all fell into place for me. Access to capital is the magic ingredient allowing even the poorest person to make better business choices. Microfinance simply makes good sense. Two important corollary points are worth noting:

1. Borrowers highly value their loans and usually try to get one or more follow-up loans. This means borrowers typically believe they are reaping substantial benefits from the loans — a powerful testament to the potential benefits of this system.

2. The penalty exacted by an MFI is less menacing than the threat of physical violence from the local loan shark. If a loan is not paid back to a microfinance institution, the penalties are loss of respect in the community, the ineligibility for follow-up loans, and the costs to co-guarantors who are required to pay back the loan. Those are significant costs to be sure, yet pale in comparison to harsh physical harm or a child being handed over for slave labor.

ASPECTS OF SCALE

Microfinance institutions can benefit from operating at larger scales. One advantage of organizing a sophisticated microfinance infrastructure is that it can be replicated rather easily. It is possible for one MFI to have central offices in many countries and for those central offices to service branch offices and community banks in thousands of locations. Some of the large networks of MFIs — such as Accion International, FINCA International, Hope International, and Opportunity International — serve hundreds of thousands or millions of borrowers around the world.

Another potential benefit of size is the percentage of the cost of overhead compared to income shrinks as organizations grow. When this happens, the organization can use more of its resources to help poor people. Larger MFIs are also more easily able to offer other financial services, such as savings accounts and insurance. As noted in previous chapters, the poor often value the opportunity to save much more than the opportunity to borrow.

In many countries, an MFI must be a regulated financial entity before borrowers are allowed to have savings accounts. The process of becoming regulated is usually expensive and time consuming. An MFI is often required to have several million dollars in capital and become a for-profit entity instead of a nonprofit entity. However, savings accounts not only benefit the borrowers; they offer a huge benefit for the MFI. Once an MFI is able to offer savings accounts, it typically gains the right to use the savings accounts as a source of loan funds to other borrowers. Consequently, many MFIs value this new source of lending capital because it keeps them from having to raise money from unpredictable donors or borrow from commercial sources.

TRENDS AND EVENTS

Successful and expanding MFIs are primarily driven by the desire to lend increasing amounts of money and to provide better services. Sometimes these desires work together and sometimes they are in conflict. Note the paradoxes when we look at the possible sources of loan capital for MFIs:

Donors: Donors want MFIs to have low overhead rates and provide many services to poor people. However, low overhead rates typically mean the MFI needs to grow larger, spend more money raising money, and reduce the number of services it offers. Individual donors are hard to find and hard to count on for the long term. This makes it difficult for a growing MFI to count on donor funds.

Profits: An MFI can generate additional money to lend by having profit. However, profits often improve by increasing interest rates and/or reducing services to borrowers.

Commercial Sources: An MFI can increase the size of its loan portfolio by borrowing money from outside commercial sources. These sources might include commercial banks, professional investors, foundations, and mutual funds. These commercial sources are, in turn, driven by the need to be repaid and make a profit, so they tend to push MFIs to increase interest rates and reduce services. Although there is a cost to MFIs to have this money, it is often easier and cheaper to access than donor money and can usually be accessed in very large amounts.

Recent events in microfinance demonstrate how these trends play out:

- In 2007, the Mexican microfinance group Banco Compartamos completed an initial public offering, selling 30 percent ownership of the bank. The existing investors received $450 million. Based on its extremely high profit margins, this for-profit organization commanded a market value of $1.4 billion. While some lauded its success, others berated the shareholders for being greedy and taking advantage of poor people who had no other source for loans.

- SKS is an MFI in India. It has taken advantage of the willingness of Indian banks, the private equity market, and other commercial sources to loan money to MFIs. It is now sufficiently capitalized to add ten thousand new borrowers *per month.*

- Fonkoze, an MFI located in Haiti, starts two community banks a month at a cost of $50,000 each. On average, each community bank is self-sufficient after one year and can begin repaying its loan capitalization. Fonkoze recently borrowed money in order to start a large number of these banks. Without the ability to borrow money, Fonkoze would have to grow at a much slower pace.

- UPS awarded $1 million to three microfinance organizations, announcing, "There could be no better way to celebrate founder Jim Casey's entrepreneurial spirit than to award grants to foster opportunities for entrepreneurs around the world."[5]

These types of funding did not start occurring until a few years ago.

Prior to that, funding from individual donors was the primary source of MFI capitalization.

In the end, the beneficiaries of microfinance are poor people who improve their lives. A Ukrainian laborer, Vladimir Ghovhashev, exemplifies the benefits to be gained from microfinance. He has received eight microloans which have been invested in his small iron-manufacturing business. He plans to invest his latest loan in a second workshop for manufacturing iron railings, grates, fences, pokers, and frames. Vladimir's skill in this age-old craft has helped his business grow and succeed, but he couldn't have done it without access to capital via microloans. His loans have helped him save money by purchasing material at volume discounts. He now works alongside a team of three employees, helping them provide for their families too. As a single father, Vladimir's primary responsibility is meeting the needs of his young son, but beyond that, Vladimir has improved his community by donating to the Ukrainian Association for the Visually Handicapped and making a roof for the local Baptist church.

Microfinance has become a well-accepted technique to reduce poverty in developing countries around the world. To summarize, microfinance allows the following:

- Outside capital flows into poor communities, stimulating additional economic activity.
- Funds are recycled to other borrowers within the community, maximizing the impact of funds.
- Borrowers typically improve their incomes on a long-term basis.
- Programs can be replicated to serve many borrowers.

If microfinance did nothing more than this, it would be an exceptionally powerful technique to alleviate poverty. However, many MFIs and donors recognize that the "theme" of microfinance described in this chapter is just the beginning.

8

EXPLORING VARIATIONS IN MICROFINANCE 2.0

(PETER)

When you sing "Twinkle, Twinkle, Little Star" to your child at bedtime, you might be unaware that this simple melody was the basis for a Mozart piano masterpiece. In "Variations on *Ah vous dirai-je, Maman*," Mozart takes a simple theme and creates twelve complex and beautiful variations that challenge accomplished pianists. In a similar way, we have described the core methodologies of savings and credit associations and microfinance institutions and their "theme" of how accessing capital unlocks productivity. But this is just the beginning. This chapter shows the incredible variations possible through microfinance. Think of it as microfinance 2.0.

Microfinance institutions currently reach over 100 million entrepreneurs and their families.[1] This is an extensive network. If each entrepreneur is a member of a family averaging five persons, 500 million people are in regular contact with organizations purportedly focused on improving their lives. Innovators recognize that this vast distribution channel has the capacity to provide many other valuable services to the poor.

Variations on the theme of microfinance are pushing the boundaries — with several innovative "products" that are reaching beggars, youth, and even prostitutes.

CELL PHONES

One of the first successes in expanding the boundaries within microfinance was orchestrated by Mohammed Yunus and Iqbal Qadir in Bangladesh with Grameen Phone. In 1995, Grameen Bank had already established a network of more than two million entrepreneurs spread over 35,000 villages and was anxious to see what it could accomplish next. Yunus and Qadir recognized that knowing the current market price for commodities could greatly enhance the bargaining power of poor farmers, and that a three-minute phone call could save hours for a merchandiser who needs to know if her goods have arrived in a nearby city. Propelled by the communications revolution of the 1990s, they realized poor villagers around the world could access a wealth of information via cell phones if only they had access. Select Grameen clients were given a loan to purchase a cell phone. In an environment where there are very few phones and financially there is no way each villager could afford a phone of her own, the "cell phone ladies" became a key part of the community's commercial activity while also growing a thriving small business. Think of it as the Bangladeshi version of the pay phones that were commonly seen at gas stations, airports, and restaurants in our country until everyone had their own cell phone.[2]

Others have followed Grameen Phone's example. Urwego in Rwanda began working with the Grameen Foundation in 2006 to provide "phone loans" to existing clients located in rural areas. These loans are used to purchase a village phone kit from Mobile Telephone Networks (MTN) that includes a cable and extended antenna to be placed in a tall tree or pole in the village as well as an earpiece and a car battery for charging the phone.[3] Marie-Claire Ayurwanda is one of the entrepreneurs who is benefiting from this innovative partnership. She was a client of Urwego who initially received a loan to open a small restaurant she called Isimbi. She took an additional loan to purchase the phone kit and repaid the loan in only five months. She sells approximately thirty minutes of airtime per day to her community, providing about $12 of profit each week. In Rwanda, where the average income is only $230 per year, this extra income is having a significant effect on Marie-Claire's family.[4]

MICRO-INSURANCE

According to the Census Bureau's 2007 Current Population Survey, 47 million US citizens live without insurance.[5] Lack of health care is a serious *problem* in the U.S.; it is a *crisis* in many parts of the world. Exact statistics are difficult to find, but anecdotally, I have never found an individual living anywhere near the poverty line who had any formal insurance unless it was through an MFI. As you would expect, insurance is a luxury that most poor people cannot afford.

While companies like Allianz AG and State Farm Insurance Companies span the globe, their services seldom (if ever) reach the poor and the marginalized in the developing world. But so what? How important *is* insurance? From a business standpoint, would the poor even be willing to pay for insurance if it were available?

For the poor, health insurance is actually of critical importance because it would provide some protection from emergencies. Instead of a broken leg and subsequent infection pushing an already poor person into destitution, insurance could allow a trip to the city for a clean cast and a pair of crutches. The collective microfinance network provides a way to cost-effectively provide insurance to the very poor in remote parts of the world.

Margarie is a client in Trou du Nord, Haiti, who is on her second loan cycle with Esperanza. She owns and operates a restaurant near a busy walkway and sells rice, soup, and black beans from three pots she bought with her first loan. Every entrepreneur who receives a loan from Esperanza is also covered by their health insurance plan; it is a benefit for all borrowers. Margarie and her family now have free semiannual medical checkups

and long-term health care. This wasn't always available. Prior to joining Esperanza, Margarie would deposit regular "premiums" in a small jar she buried in the ground in anticipation of some medical emergency. Margarie now has safe, reliable, and consistent access to health care services that she said has made a "huge impact on my life ... now I know I can help my family."

In February 2008, the Bill and Melinda Gates Foundation awarded a $24.2 million grant to Opportunity International's subsidiary, the Micro Insurance Agency (MIA), to significantly expand its insurance products to the poor in Africa, Asia, and Latin America. MIA has enabled the world's first stand-alone micro-insurance agency and is poised to enter eleven new countries and provide life, health, and crop insurance to 21 million poor people by 2012.[6] Health insurance premiums for a family of five average $1.50 per month, which is often included as part of their loan payment.

This price and delivery mechanism makes insurance affordable for individuals living on the continent of Africa, where only 0.3 percent of the poor are currently insured.[7]

Micro-insurance includes a range of products that can help the working poor manage economic hardship such as flooding, drought, hospitalization, or a death in the family. Workers in the developing world are more likely to experience hardship that can trap them in lifelong poverty, yet less than 3 percent of people in the world's one hundred poorest countries have any type of insurance.[8]

By using their microfinance platform, Opportunity International can effectively provide insurance by either charging small monthly fees or withholding portions of the loan disbursements to clients. The growth of this initiative has been impressive: Micro Insurance Agency has over 675,000 policies covering 3.3 million lives.[9]

On the ground, such programs are affordable and convenient. Mara, a thirty-one-year-old mother of four, lives in East Timor. Mara pays 5 percent of her loan amount as payment for her insurance premium. This payment is easily covered through her increased business income. She is glad to make the payment because it means that she and her children have regular access to preventive health and even dental services. More important, however, Mara knows that in the event of an emergency, insurance will protect her family from disaster. A microloan gives Mara daily hope and income, while micro-insurance piggybacked on that loan gives her daily peace of mind about her family's health and financial future.

LIFE SKILLS EDUCATION

This morning when I was eating Cheerios with my daughter, I studied the back of the box. When I was growing up, the backs of cereal boxes were the place for brightly colored matching games, mazes, and interesting facts about the world. Now this space is used for something very different —

advertising. And not advertising for other General Mills cereals, either, but for Pampers Cruisers. The marketing team at Pampers knows that the back of a Cheerios box is a great way to reach a key demographic — parents of young children.

In a similar way, microfinance institutions have recognized they can reach a captive audience and transmit important messages that could improve the lives of their clientele. Credit with Education, as it is commonly referred, takes advantage of the weekly/biweekly meeting structure of microfinance. A leader in the Credit with Education movement, Free-

dom from Hunger provides training and technical assistance in health, nutrition, and business and household finance to clients of microfinance institutions around the world.[10]

Microfinance institutions are utilizing their reach to inform clients and their communities about everything from business training to the benefits of breast-feeding, from labor codes to language skills. Clients and those in their communities can learn to be healthier, productive citizens. When integrated with the church, this can deepen relationships that point people to Christ.

When Urwego's clients in Rwanda meet for their weekly repayments, they receive biblically based business training. This training had a powerful impact on one woman who had a diseased cow. Euthanizing the cow would have resulted in significant losses for her, so she tried to bribe a butcher to slaughter the cow despite its sickness, so that she could sell the meat to unsuspecting customers. Before following through with this plan, however, she participated in a biblical training session on ethics. She recognized the harmful impact of her plan, told her group about her change of intent, and was quick to point out that the training is what made the difference in her behavior.

MICRO-PHARMACIES

On my last trip to Haiti, I either ate some food or drank some water that caused me severe abdominal pain. After two days of living in the bathroom, doctors informed me that I had shigellosis, also known as bacillary dysentery. As soon as we received this diagnosis, my wife ran off to CVS to pick up a prescription for an antibiotic called ciprofloxacin. After popping a few pills, I was back to normal, with only a sore backside to remind me of my illness.

When I had this illness, I never once feared for my life. In the United States, it is virtually unheard of to perish from this illness, simply because medicine exists. But I was shocked to learn that shigellosis causes more than one million deaths each year, mostly in children in the developing world. Mothers and fathers across the globe are mourning the needless loss of their children. The problem is getting affordable medicine to the nearly three thousand people dying each day. Microfinance institutions can be instrumental in making this happen by leveraging their networks to provide basic health services and access to medicine such as simple antibiotics.

The Center for Community Transformation (CCT) was established in 1992 to provide an organized and systematic response to poverty eradication and spiritual transformation in the Philippines. In its never-ending innovation, CCT now operates an optical and pharmaceutical drug center, called Generic Pharmacy, which offers eye checkups, glasses, and drugs to clients at dramatically reduced prices.[11] When the franchise launched in 2007, about twenty stores opened in the greater Manila area. By May 10, 2008, this number exceeded 140 franchise locations country-wide as CCT leveraged its reach to extend affordable drugs and free medical consultations.

Another pioneer in this pursuit to distribute generic medicines to those in need is The HealthStore Foundation. Founded by Scott Hillstrom to address the lack of medical services around the world, The HealthStore Foundation has established a network of micro-pharmacies and clinics whose mission is to provide access to essential medicines to marginalized populations in the developing world.[12] The HealthStore outlets target the most common killer diseases, including malaria, respiratory infections, and dysentery. They also provide health education and prevention services, all within a micro-franchise model called CFWshops (Child & Family Wellness Shops). These franchises are entitled to receive a supply of high-quality and low-cost drugs, management support, training, and other valuable benefits from HealthStore to ensure the standardization and success of the program.[13]

Both of these models have relationships with microfinance institutions that help identify entrepreneurs and expand the message of these health clinics. The reality is that this new access to affordable and life-saving treatments means that when children get sick with shigellosis, they do not die.

MICRO-SCHOOLS

The U.S. Department of Health & Human Services notes that "individuals with less than a high-school education … are at the greatest risk of becoming poor, despite their work effort."[14] This insight is true in the developing world as well: *education* is a key to success.

But what if no quality schools exist in your neighborhood? Is there a social business venture that could become self-sufficient and provide this key service to the poor? Opportunity International (OI) announced in December 2007 the expansion of its microfinance school loans program, "Micro-schools for Opportunity." These micro-schools provide loans to educational entrepreneurs who open schools in poor neighborhoods where children, especially girls, would otherwise be unable to access public education. In essence, they are providing loans and training for people who open private schools around the world. Not surprisingly, parents are willing to pay for education

for their children, even in the poorest areas, because they recognize the advantages that education will provide for their kids.

Milán Tapia is an educational entrepreneur with Esperanza in the Dominican Republic. After taking her first loan in 2000, and after building a financially successful sewing business, Milán wanted to pass on her blessings to others. She focused on her community's children, especially those who were particularly disadvantaged. She developed a vision for educating, feeding, and loving these children, providing them with an *hogar Cristiano* (Christian home). Her school began with few students, but soon community members began bringing more children to her, many of whom lived on the streets. Milán became a teacher, mentor, and mother to these children. By 2007, *Tu Hogar Christiano* served roughly two hundred children each day and with Esperanza's assistance is becoming a viable business that will meet the educational needs of these children for years to come.

CORPORATE PIGGYBACKING

According to United Nations surveys between 1995 and 2003, nearly half of sub-Saharan children under the age of five suffer from stunted growth, a marker of malnutrition and a harbinger of physical and mental challenges.[15] To combat this crisis, several microfinance institutions are creating partnerships that address basic nutritional needs. Once again, Muhammad Yunus in Bangladesh is leading in innovation and pioneering programs that will have relevance in Africa and other parts of the developing world. He initiated a joint venture with yogurt manufacturer Dannon Company to bring healthy daily nutrition to low-income populations in Bangladesh.[16] Known as Grameen Dannon Foods, this joint venture is registered as a social business enterprise in which all profits are invested back into the company or the communities it serves. The widespread infrastructure of Grameen Bank allows life-saving products to be quickly disseminated and distributed throughout Bangladesh.

Another example of a corporate partnership occurred between the Center for Community Transformation (CCT) and Pepsi-Cola. Insufficient potable water is a serious issue in Manila, the fifth largest city in the world and home to over nineteen million people. Water from the taps is unsafe and water merchants charge exorbitant prices, forcing the poor to drink contaminated water.

To solve this problem, CCT came up with an innovative solution. The center persuaded Pepsi to donate a state-of-the-art water purification system. CCT located the water purification system in the middle of one of the poorest slums in Manila, right next to a water merchant who was charging a day's wage for a day's water. The water produced by the CCT-Pepsi water system is so clean that they proudly point out, "Even babies can drink it." CCT charges for the water, but it is a reasonable amount that everyone in the slum can afford. It pays a commission to a group of homeless men who deliver the large jugs of water to people throughout the slum. CCT uses the gray water that is not drinkable to provide a laundry service for the people. In conjunction with the credit cooperative, local entrepreneurs sell detergents and provide laundry services for community members.

SMALL AND MEDIUM ENTERPRISES

While most microfinance efforts focus on the poor, there are other entrepreneurs ready for larger amounts of capital for their small- or medium-size businesses who are unable to obtain traditional loans from conventional banks. Loans over $5,000 are necessary for some entrepreneurs to achieve economies of scale and more rapidly expand a business. These loans help to build a productive middle class and expand employment opportunities. Microfinance institutions are helping these larger entrepreneurs, either by expanding the size of their loans or creating linkages with formal banks and "handing off" entrepreneurs that outgrow the MFI.

During low tide in Cap Haitian Bay off the coast of Haiti, near the city of Trou du Nord, local residents explain that you can see portions of the shipwrecked Santa Maria, one of the three ships sailed by Columbus. Despite its great historical allure, you won't find much destination tourism here. Haiti was ranked by *Forbes* magazine in 2008 as the fourth most dangerous country in the world (behind Somalia, Iraq, and Afghanistan), and it is the poorest country in the Western Hemisphere.

When I visited this rural part of Haiti, I met a woman named Iva Dulorier. An enterprising entrepreneur, Iva is as adventurous and ambitious as the captain of the Santa Maria and is experiencing great success in the shadow of the famous boat. Iva produces salt. With her microloan, Iva purchased shovels and other equipment to build canals that lead inland from the sea to small thirty-by-thirty-foot pools. These pools fill with seawater during high tide. Iva then closes the canals, trapping the water. Over time, the water evaporates, leaving mounds of salt deposits that she col-

lects, sells to factories, and saves. Iva has found a simple, though carefully calculated, way to make money on such a readily available commodity.

Iva has expanded her business and now provides seasonal employment for *thirty* people. In less than two years, she has become a leading employer and businesswoman in her community. She is ready to launch into a shrimp business and recently applied for a medium-size loan through the SME department of the microfinance institution to secure the necessary equipment.

Not every entrepreneur achieves this level of success, but entrepreneurs like Iva are ready for larger amounts of capital to continue to capitalize their businesses.

HOUSING

Pedro Lacen grew up in an impoverished family just outside Santo Domingo, the capital city of the Dominican Republic. He spent his youth in a shack with a dirt floor and a leaky roof. Perhaps this is the reason Pedro is so enthusiastic about his current position with Esperanza; Pedro is responsible for housing improvement loans. The Firm Foundation program is Esperanza's newest innovation, centered on the belief that people can lead more productive, healthy lives if they are not worried about their home collapsing or their belongings becoming wet and moldy. Loans are used to buy materials to lay cement flooring and construct a watertight roof. Usually larger than most business loans, these loans have a repayment period of three years.

After being prescreened for the ability to repay a housing improvement loan, recipients of this program are chosen through their community banks (called "Bank of Hope") in order of greatest need. Local community bank members in turn donate their time and efforts to make these improvements happen, benefiting the community in two important ways: (a) an increased sense of solidarity within the community and (b) increased

home values within the greater community. In addition, families often feel a strong sense of pride — it is not uncommon to see other home improvements follow in the wake of the new floors. Pedro mentions that clients are now painting the exterior of their homes, taking greater care to remove trash, and helping their neighbors with similar improvement projects.

AGRICULTURAL FINANCE

In 2002, the Consultative Group to Assist the Poor (CGAP) received funding from the International Fund for Agricultural Development (IFAD) to conduct research on the feasibility of financing small-scale agricultural efforts. They discovered that most microfinance institutions were not meeting the needs of the agricultural sector. The reasons were obvious: delivery of services to rural areas is expensive, population density is low, economies of scale were difficult to achieve, and loans were so small that it was difficult to cover costs through interest rates. CGAP summarized the findings this way:

> Agricultural finance is notoriously risky. Many farmers need credit to purchase seeds and other inputs, as well as to harvest, process, market and transport their crops. While borrowing on the basis of anticipated crop production might seem logical where collateral assets are few, such loans expose the lender to production and price risk. Natural disaster, a decline in market prices, unexpectedly low yields, the lack of a buyer, or loss due to poor storage conditions are only some of the factors that can result in lower-than-expected revenues. Such a fall in revenues can often lead to high default rates on agricultural loans. The overwhelming failure of state development banks that provided billions of dollars in subsidized agricultural finance to farmers in the 1970s and 1980s, combined with scant rural penetration by risk-averse commercial financial institutions, has led to a widespread dearth of agricultural credit. Yet, new approaches are increasingly being developed to fill this gap in a sustainable and efficient manner.[17]

Despite these daunting challenges to agricultural lending and savings, individuals are showing that there are economic development opportunities within agriculture. Agros International is a Seattle-based nonprofit that works with poor landless farmers in Central America and Mexico. Agros takes a variation on microfinance by extending loans for purchases of farmland, then partnering with farmers in applying sustainable agricultural practices, all with the goal of enabling these families to create, develop, and eventually own their own farms.[18]

Mario is one of the farmers benefiting from Agros training and small loans in Nicaragua. Based on the advice of the visiting agronomist and in partnership with Agros, he ventured beyond the traditional plantains and planted beans, squash, papaya, and watermelon. In the first year, Mario sold approximately $62 of squash alone. Considering the normal wage for a day laborer in Nicaragua is approximately $1.50 per day, Mario has been making a substantial profit on the squash and other fruits and vegetables. He is expanding his agricultural efforts, taking better care of the soil, and strengthening his family's finances.[19]

CLEAN WATER

After Yakalakshmi's entire family fell sick from drinking water directly from the tap in her village of Nekkunda in Andhra Pradesh, India, and after she had to spend $100 to treat the ensuing illnesses, she enthusiastically welcomed innovative ways to provide clean water for her family. So when Yakalakshmi was given an opportunity to buy an effective water purifier through her Self Help Group on an installment basis, she was quick to subscribe.

Yakalakshmi is among the many beneficiaries of a unique partnership between ACCESS Development Services, an Indian microfinance technical services nonprofit, and Hindustan Unilever Limited (HUL), one of the country's largest producers of consumer goods, to provide safe drinking water to the rural poor. HUL has designed a household water purifier, PureIt, which uses a four-stage filtration process to remove all bacteria, viruses, dirt, and pesticides, resulting in water that is sanitary and safe to drink. This purifier doesn't require electricity or running water. To purchase these purifiers, ACCESS facilitates loans through its partner microfinance institutions for rural women who need them most, like Yakalakshmi.[20]

PEOPLE

Microfinance is not just developing new products to assist the global poor; it is targeting new and diverse poor populations left behind by traditional economic assistance. Many people believe that microfinance works only for entrepreneurs who have existing businesses, but this assumption is being challenged. Consider the following examples of the lives of beggars, youth, and prostitutes being improved by innovative microfinance initiatives.

BEGGARS

Since Yunus and his Grameen Bank received the Nobel Peace Prize in 2006, microfinance has continued to gain momentum and exposure. However, this increased exposure has also attracted critics who question whether microfinance is reaching the poorest of the poor.

Grameen Bank started a program exclusively for beggars called the Struggling Beggar Members Program. For Yunus, this was a simple way to test his hypothesis that "all human beings are born entrepreneurs. Some get a chance to unleash that capacity. Some never got the chance, never knew that he or she has that capacity."[21]

Grameen loan officers visit beggars on the streets of Bangladesh and explain that a better life is possible than their hand-to-mouth existence. Loan officers explain that beggars could easily begin a simple business. "As you go from house to house, would you take some merchandise with you — some cookies, some candy, some toys, some sweets?"[22] As beggars began consenting and subscribing to these beggar loans — typically no more than $15, repayable without interest, designed as start-up capital for an elementary micro-business — Yunus realized how powerful this mobilized force could be. These de facto door-to-door salespersons, already equipped with sales know-how, were now equipped with the capital to truly profit from their skills rather than simply survive. The incentive to repay these zero-interest loans was the opportunity of receiving consecutive loans upon successful repayment. Today, Grameen Bank has served over 100,000 beggars, more than ten thousand of whom have risen from begging into other employment. Of the other ninety thousand, Yunus likes to claim that they are probably only part-time beggars in the process of kind of closing down their begging division and concentrating on their sales division.[23]

In the Philippines, the Center for Community Transformation (CCT) also found an innovative way to care for the poorest of the poor. *Pulúbi*, or "beggars" in Tagalog, have few opportunities to escape poverty. Manila is a megacity to which people from all over the Philippines move in hopes of finding a job and a better life. Unfortunately, finding sustainable employment is difficult, and many of these hardworking rural transplants are forced to live on the streets. CCT began a visitation ministry to these people and quickly realized their capacity for productive employment. CCT invited a few to come to their offices to work on a temporary basis, and soon these few beggars became full-time employees. CCT eventually hired twenty *pulúbi* as full-time employees, who were able to leave the streets and live dignified lives.

However, twenty employees was scarcely a dent in the serious problem of the street dwellers. CCT realized that if the *pulúbi* were good enough to work for them, they would be good enough to work for anyone. Several nearby companies had basic needs for cleaners and cooks but could not afford full-time staff. So CCT started a temporary work agency to supply *pulúbi* to local companies for one to three days a week. The temp agency is structured as a cooperative in partnership with microfinance services. In addition to their daily wages, the *pulúbi* employees have ownership shares and receive annual dividends based on profitability. No longer does CCT refer to these hardworking indiviuals as *pulúbi*, but as *kaibigan*, or friends.

Impoverished individuals caught at the lowest levels of society, when given access to capital, legitimate employment possibilities, and the belief that improvement is possible, are able to live new lives through entrepreneurship.

YOUTH

Compassion International and other leading Christian proponents of child sponsorship faced a startling realization. They were helping children receive an education, improving their nutrition, and developing their communities. However, what happened when these children "graduated" from the child-sponsorship model at age eighteen? Only a small number had an opportunity to attend university, and even fewer had options for formal employment. In many countries, starting a small business is often a person's only option for employment. Was there a role here for microfinance and employment opportunities to help youth make this transition?

YouthWorks founder Audrey Codera wanted to ease the transition youth face when transitioning to adulthood. She recognized that although microfinance was flourishing in the Philippines, there were few opportunities for youth to benefit from small loans and savings services. She solicited family and friends to help provide the start-up capital for three underprivileged youth who had solid business plans. After these three loans were repaid, she recognized that entrepreneurial youth can effectively start small businesses and should not be cut off from the burgeoning microfinance movement. YouthWorks was born and is currently providing employment opportunities for over three hundred youth. Amazingly, from the inception in 2006, the repayment rate for all microloans is 100 percent, helping to disprove the notion that microfinance does not work with youth.[24]

PROSTITUTES

On Valentine's Day in Rwanda, I had an unusual visitor at my home. A prostitute must have known that I was a single American living alone in Kigali, and she came knocking to see if I might be interested in some

company. What I *was* interested in was finding a way to help her earn a living without having to sell her body.

The "world's oldest profession" is evidence that some women feel so desperate that they will do whatever it takes to survive and provide for their families. If you were living in poverty with children to feed and no prospects for employment, what would you do, particularly when you had a "job" that you knew would pay a sufficient amount? Countless women and children are forced into this form of slavery and often see no way out.

For many women in prostitution, entrepreneurship offers an alternative. If these women know how to sell, why can't it be a product other than their bodies? A Kenyan girl lamented, "I may have to go into prostitution, and then I know I will get HIV and die; I would rather have a real business, but it is not easy."[25]

But what if we could offer hope for the future and a pathway out of poverty? Esperanza identified fifteen women (mostly Haitian) who were involved in prostitution in Puerto Plata, Dominican Republic, to pilot a new program called Forty Days to a New Life. "Someone had to show care for them," notes Executive Director Carlos Pimental. "They're in prostitution because of poverty." Esperanza uses the curriculum developed in Rick Warren's *The Purpose Driven Life* to lead these women through a forty-day renewal process. Esperanza then introduces microfinance, business training, and alternative income sources through entrepreneurship. Just two months after the process began, many came to know Jesus Christ, most turned their backs on prostitution, and several took a loan from Esperanza to begin a new life.

IT'S TIME TO CHANGE THE WORLD

Sometimes a small discovery has the potential to change the world. Is it possible that microfinance has started a revolution to radically reshape the way we address severe poverty? We now see the poor not as objects of charity but as coparticipants in the vital work of economic development and global change. Microfinance may be the simple, beautiful theme from which variations continue to unfold in wonderful complexity.

Jared Diamond writes in *Guns, Germs and Steel* that civilizations located at crossroads always develop more rapidly than societies isolated by geographic factors such as rivers and mountains. Our society — indeed our world — now exists at a global crossroads of information and possibility.

Given the flexibility, simplicity, and power of microfinance, a dramatic reduction in poverty is a realistic goal.

9

IT CAN'T BE THAT GOOD,
CAN IT?

(PETER)

Given the merits of microfinance and Savings and Credit Associations, it would be tempting to see these as *the* tools for ending global poverty, as *the* tools with which the church can address physical and spiritual needs in every situation. This chapter is meant to temper any unrealistic expectations you might have about microfinance and SCAs. Sometimes exuberance for the observed results of microfinance causes its advocates to place that method on too high a pedestal. We must be frank and thoughtful about the shortcomings and limitations of microfinance, lest we expect too much of it.[1]

WHAT DO WE WANT:
ERADICATION OR ALLEVIATION?

Some of the most ardent microfinance supporters suggest that it will eliminate poverty. Nobel Peace Prize winner Muhammad Yunus believes Bangladesh will be free of poverty by 2030 and has even said, "I say let's build a poverty museum, because that's the only place you'll be able to see [poverty]."[2] Statements such as this are effective rallying cries. Indeed, development skeptics need this kind of vision, yet over-exuberance may raise

expectations to an unattainable and unrealistic level. Statements like these may fuel skepticism among academics as questions emerge about whether microfinance will have a lasting impact on poverty.

Asserting that the goal of microfinance is poverty *alleviation* is quite different from asserting that the goal is poverty *eradication.* Many studies of microfinance clients have shown increases and diversification in income and assets and decreases in vulnerability. Even though anecdotal evidence shows it is possible to make large gains, large enough to eradicate that instance of poverty, studies show that the norm is more modest — alleviation. Would a 100 percent increase in an income of $1 per day *eradicate* a family's poverty? Or would even a 500 percent increase? No, but it would *alleviate* their poverty and make their lives much better.

A 100 percent increase in income, even from one dollar to two, means a family eats better, enjoys better health, improves their housing, and has greater confidence and hope for the future. Increased income can radically transform local churches as the giving of members increases. An increase in income can provide a catalytic boost toward additional improvement — perhaps even permanent escape from poverty. The stories of some clients may not appear dramatic to those in wealthy nations and may not even register as a blip on a country's gross national product (GNP). But for the people earning a dollar a day, a second dollar can make a huge difference — pocket change to us, but the world to them.

The vast majority of microfinance clients are benefiting in real and unprecedented ways. A tempered understanding of the impact of microfinance will help ensure new ways of expanding outreach to the millions who have yet to take advantage of this powerful tool while at the same time protecting us from the damaging delusion that microfinance will simply erase all of the world's financial problems.

MICROFINANCE CAN CAUSE HARM

Unlike other forms of aid, microfinance is not an end product. While a bag of rice is the solution for immediate hunger, microfinance is an *opportunity*, not a total *solution*. When an organization distributes rice in a neighborhood, families enjoy the end benefit of the project: food for the table. With microfinance, the client receives one ingredient, capital, in the broader recipe of income generation. The additional ingredients of time, work, and (often) an existing enterprise must be mixed with the microloan in order for the end result to be achieved. Microfinance is a single step — albeit a very important one — in the process of poverty alleviation.

Not every microfinance client enjoys dramatic success. A small percentage fail — a reality in every market economy. Individuals eager to discredit microfinance might dramatize these isolated examples and ignore the benefits obtained by the vast majority of microfinance clients. Yet even though harm is not the norm (nearly every MFI is focused on seeing their clients succeed), it is instructive to note some of the ways in which microfinance can fail and to remember that such failures represent human lives still trapped in poverty.

Mama Beatrice heard of a promising opportunity in a district outside the capital of Kinshasa, Democratic Republic of the Congo. The rumor mill said that coffee beans could be sold profitably and quickly in this region due to the high cost of transportation and the fluctuating scarcity of certain goods. So, sight unseen, she took out a microloan and invested her capital in coffee beans that she planned to sell outside Kinshasa. Unfortunately, the business rumors were just rumors; it took her months, not days, to sell her stock of coffee beans, and she was barely able to meet her loan payments. Instead of continuing to work at her marginally profitable business as a basic shopkeeper, using her loan in that business, she ventured into an unsuccessful business based on a rumor and her desire for a quick profit.

Galina and her daughter owned a small business selling clothing in a local market in Ukraine. They had been successful borrowers for two years and proved to be honest and responsible entrepreneurs. Hoping to expand their business, they left the local market and rented a storefront to become a "department store." Using two $2,000 loans, they purchased new winter clothing and expected good sales. Unfortunately, the following winter was unseasonably warm and the income from their sparse sales covered only part of their rent payments. The landlord confiscated their goods and forced them to leave.

Problems can arise when microloans are misused or when the borrower fails to fully evaluate external risks that are universal to business. Sometimes, a borrower seems to have no fault, yet still fails. In rare cases, the borrower is worse off for having taken out a microloan. But none of these cases impugn the usefulness of microfinance as a powerful tool. Borrowing is inherently risky, and despite the best efforts of those involved, a small percentage of microfinance ventures will fail.

Realistically, failure to pay back loans is relatively rare among the very poor. Instead, the client success rate is tremendously high, perhaps because microfinance clients have already been tested and toughened. Before microfinance enters a village, there are few options. Most likely, the only source of capital in town is a loan shark who charges exorbitant rates, yet many among the poor are *still* able to operate somewhat profitable businesses. It is no wonder most borrowers embrace microfinance loans and succeed in a new, more nurturing financial environment.

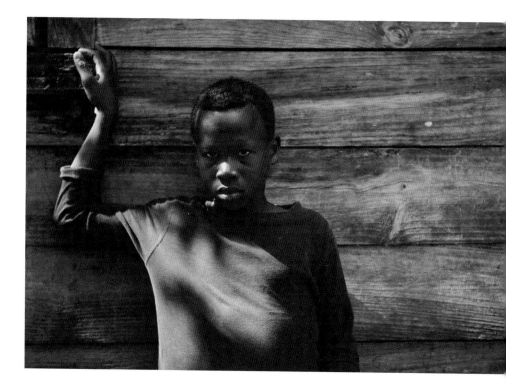

MICROFINANCE IS NOT FOR EVERYONE

Some people are born entrepreneurs, while others seem to lack the drive or talent to use capital effectively. Those who lack entrepreneurial skills might make honest, hardworking employees at factories, hotels, and other income-generating businesses, but very few opportunities for these types of jobs likely exist locally.

When Westerners wonder how it is possible that so many hundreds of thousands of clients are clamoring for business loans, keep in mind that the economy in a developing country is dramatically different than it is in a country like the United States. In many places, formal employment opportunities simply do not exist, even at what we would consider the most menial levels. There are no fast-food restaurants like McDonald's or Taco Bell, no retail chains like Wal-Mart, and few factories that hire

manual laborers. White-collar jobs are even more scarce. The complex legal environment and government instability typically found in developing countries discourage foreign investment and compound the shortage of employment opportunities. In these situations, a person who wants to make money has almost no option other than self-employment. A worker's alternative isn't a boring job at a warehouse or sitting on the porch and waiting for an unemployment check — it is destitution.

Survival is a powerful impetus for individuals to try to sell whatever they can. A woman will bake a few extra loaves of bread to sell on the street, or a man will hawk a leather belt and a pair of shoes. In fact, many microfinance loans finance income-generating activities that supplement, rather than replace, family incomes earned from day labor, agriculture, or other seasonal income. If company jobs were as scarce in America as they are in Africa — and self-employment were the only option — there is no question that we would be a nation of street vendors and small-scale entrepreneurs, especially if the government did not provide social safety nets.

MICROFINANCE IS BUT ONE PIECE OF DEVELOPMENT

From a development viewpoint, there is a level of need below the threshold that microfinance can reach. Grants and emergency care are needed in post-conflict and post-disaster situations since people can focus on longer-term issues, such as employment, only after their immediate needs are addressed.

From a financial viewpoint, microfinance provides part of the foundation upon which to build communities, but there also needs to be the next level of small- and medium-size enterprises as well as large corporations. All these work together, and the more a country advances, the greater the opportunities for large-scale investments.

From a spiritual viewpoint, there is a critical need for further training of pastoral staff to teach congregations how to responsibly handle increasing

financial resources and how to live out the gospel in every area of their lives. Economic prosperity will not automatically lead to significant community and church improvement — in fact, the opposite can occur.

Lasting change and development require significant structural changes. Without a system of justice, corrupt leadership like Zimbabwe's President Robert Mugabe can literally destroy all the benefits of small-scale economic development in a day, as he did during Operation Murambatsvina (translated "cleaning up the trash"). Police bulldozed whole communities, including homes and businesses. According to the United Nations, this operation was used to punish political opponents and left 1.5 million people homeless.[3]

Such injustices must be addressed, along with land reform, access to clean water, educational system improvements, eradication of malaria, and many other critical issues.

MICROFINANCE IS CHANGING

Gatherings for microfinance practitioners have changed dramatically over the past several years — a change easily seen in the participants' shoes. A colleague commented that when he started attending microfinance forums, Birkenstocks were the footwear of choice, but now he's more likely to see polished Salvatore Ferragamo loafers. There is no question that the sector has been "professionalized" and attracts a host of entrants from the banking and finance world.

One consequence is that there is a growing push in microfinance to focus not only on sustainability and aiding the poor but on maximizing profit and shareholder return. If this trend continues, it's possible that the distribution of other services such as business and health education — key strengths of microfinance — could be cut off in the name of efficiency and profit.

Financing of MFIs from commercial sources for the expansion of loan portfolios and the growth in for-profit MFIs will fuel the need to achieve low-risk financial returns. Consequently, some MFIs may be more concerned with repayment and profit potential aspects of making loans than with changing lives. Although these two goals should not be mutually exclusive, profit-maximizing financial entities could cause MFIs to have only one bottom line — profit.

Technology is rapidly changing microfinance. Loan transactions by ATM cards or by cell phones are now occurring in remote parts of the world. These and other advances in technology have the potential to reduce the perceived need for personal contact among borrowers and between loan officers and borrowers. Yet this personal contact — from the perspective of impact, education, and spiritual change — is an indispensable need.

Given these dynamic changes, MFIs that want to do more than simply deliver access to credit and savings could appear less commercially viable from a financial viewpoint, which could hinder an ability to attract investments.

POWERFUL, NOT PERFECT

Microfinance is not a perfect one-size-fits-all solution, but it *is* an incredibly effective tool to help the poor work their way out of poverty and into a better life. Some critics assert that we shouldn't focus on microfinance because it harms a small number of individuals, but this would be akin to banning penicillin. One out of five thousand individuals who takes penicillin has a severe allergic reaction, called anaphylaxis, which is fatal unless there is immediate medical intervention. Yet penicillin has saved hundreds of thousands of lives.[4] It would be wrong to consider banning penicillin; instead, we monitor its use to ensure that it is properly administered to the right patients and in a way that maximizes impact until something better is created. The same holds true for microfinance. Responsible providers regularly monitor the impact and ensure that the staff and group

members understand the "warning signs." When an individual is harmed by a microfinance loan, the provider works that much harder to make sure that next time, the loan is successful. To ensure the greatest impact, microfinance programs must guard against focusing exclusively on maximizing profit at the expense of the poor.

With microfinance such a powerful and effective tool for fighting poverty, how might the church become more involved? The answer involves examining the possibilities of fulfilling the missions of the church and of MFIs through a new kind of partnership.

10

USING THE SECOND-BEST DISTRIBUTION SYSTEM

(PHIL)

At this point, we hope you are convinced that the church's mission is to simultaneously alleviate physical and spiritual poverty. How, then, can the church unite these two critical missions? Can microfinance help the church address both physical and spiritual needs? How might a church-led microfinance institution (MFI) differ from a secular MFI? My quest to answer these questions began when I heard a tirade against the biggest charitable foundation in the world.

"The Bill and Melinda Gates Foundation may be the most important social change agent created in the last fifty years," ranted my friend. "The foundation will very likely cause important vaccines and medicines to be invented which will have the potential to change the lives of hundreds of millions of people. But I believe it will encounter the same point of frustration facing most international charities — how will these medicines be effectively distributed? Can you imagine a truck driving up to a remote African village with a loudspeaker recording of 'Come get your magic medicine! It will make your disease go away!' No, the distribution and acceptance problems will be as costly and difficult to solve as finding the solutions!"

My friend made a lot of sense — I was struck by the difficulty of the distribution problem facing those of us who want to help people living far away in desperate conditions. Although I had seen television scenes of food trucks besieged by individuals looking for food, I had never pondered the logistical problems of distributing food, medicines, and information. It is not just the difficulty of getting goods from the place of origin to distribution points, but the continuing problem of gaining the trust of potential users and educating them in the benefits of unknown products. Without good distribution and acceptance methods, no product or service will be widely used.

Virtually everybody working in international aid has witnessed this problem. One striking example was the time aid workers drove through Goma

in the Democratic Republic of the Congo after the devastating eruption of Mt. Nyiragongo. These workers indiscriminately tossed protein bars out of their vehicle while a crowd of young Congolese ran after the vehicle grabbing all they could. Some of the younger children were practically trampled as the faster and more powerful kids hoarded a disproportionate amount. As pandemonium reigned, any onlooker would wonder just how the aid workers would report their "successful" distribution to supervisors and donors in the United States. I wonder the same thing every time I see a similar scene on television.

Even a cursory examination of the acceptance problem reveals the importance of credibility and established relationships. Imagine how you would react if a minor government official or a worker from a charitable organization showed up in your town and insisted that everybody in the community immediately start taking some kind of pills. If you're like me, you would flush your pills down the toilet until you became convinced of their benefit. But if my doctor told me to take the pills, I would take them just because I trust him.

Local residents have to first acquire faith in someone coming to help or they likely won't believe the benefits of the products or the information. Poor populations typically lack the education and background to evaluate the efficacy or utility of products and information. Instead they evaluate the person or organization *bringing* the product or information. The people coming to help must establish a relationship with the locals or they will never be able to communicate the benefits of what they are offering. In the process, both sides probably will have to overcome stereotypes and cultural prejudices.

One of the significant problems that MFIs face is the failure of past charity efforts. After all, why should a villager take a loan that must be paid back when it is possible another charity might soon appear and simply give away money or goods with no strings attached? And why should a village be expected to believe an MFI will treat them fairly when other agencies seem to act in random or destructive ways? Without developing trusted relationships, an MFI will find it difficult to get an opportunity to clearly explain the opportunities and benefits it has to offer. The hopeful message of an MFI is often poisoned by earlier charity, however well-intentioned that charity effort was at the time.

When a vaccine or food supplement arrives at its destination — even if it makes it *inside* the hut of a poor person — there is no reason to assume it will be used. People must be educated about benefits, use, and reliability,

and that's not only difficult but costly. Throwing money at making better products may not help.

The most likely way to ensure acceptance is through the influence of trusted authority figures in the community or local word of mouth. That isn't easy when so many poor people in the world are highly influenced by witch doctors or other local authority figures whose importance would be greatly diminished by outside solutions. Sometimes tradition and cultural norms are wise and reliable; other times they are simply harmful and should be changed. Unfortunately, the history of outsiders coming into communities and making good changes proves not to be any more likely than coming in and making bad changes. Since we Americans are well known for arrogantly believing we know it all, we should take special care to first develop relationships with locals to make sure we don't make a situation worse because we misunderstood the problem or offered an inappropriate solution.

In 2006, the Chalmers Center signed an agreement with Freedom from Hunger, one of the most respected secular relief and development organizations in the world. This agreement allows Chalmers to integrate biblical worldview messages into extensive curricula for training very poor people in the areas of small business, household financial management, and health. The Chalmers Center is embarking on a three-year project to integrate biblical worldview messages addressing the beliefs of animism into the curricula and adapting these for strategic locations in Africa, India, China, and Latin America. Brian Fikkert, executive director of Chalmers Center, tested some of the lessons in the slums of Kampala, Uganda. In one instance, "a witch doctor came to Christ after the first lesson. She burned her 'medicines' right there on the floor of the church and prayed for God to free her from demonic influences."[1] Not only has that witch doctor been personally freed but her example has greatly enhanced the ability of Fikkert and his colleagues to distribute their information and get it accepted.

As we start examining the distribution and acceptance problems in more detail, it is useful to look at the best distribution system in the world.

THE BEST DISTRIBUTION SYSTEM IN THE WORLD

The church is the best distribution system in the world. This might not be obvious to Americans, even those living in cities with a church building in every neighborhood. The typical American church congregation has a few hundred members. Most megachurches have only a few thousand members. Even though large denominations may have tens of millions of members, most of their church congregations are influenced primarily by local leaders. Contrast this to many other churches in the world.

In Africa, there are Anglican bishops who each exercise immense authority over a million or more church members. In Korea, the Yoido Full Gospel Church, led by David Yonggi Cho, has more than 750,000 members. Chinese house church leaders may exercise some level of authority over many millions of members. All of these numbers pale in comparison to Roman Catholicism's Vatican, which exercises authority over 1.1 billion people, or to the 220 million members of the Eastern Orthodox churches.[2]

Pastor and author Rick Warren famously illustrates this principle through three maps of the Western Province of Rwanda. In the first map, three dots mark the locations of hospitals. The second map identifies the twenty-six health clinics that serve 650,000 people. The third map identifies the locations of churches — 726 dots cover the map. This visual powerfully conveys that the church has a far greater scope and scale than virtually any other social entity.

Besides being widespread, local church leadership in other countries often has much more influence over the lives of their church members than would leadership in an American church where individuality is so highly prized. American preachers and denomination leaders are typically expected to give decent sermons on Sunday morning and maybe even do a little counseling. Beyond that, most church members resist their leadership in daily affairs. It is sad but true that local American pastors are often less influential than television personalities. After all, congregations spend far less time in front of their pastor than in front of television — and the programs on the tube are often more entertaining and memorable.

In contrast, church leaders in other countries often have tremendous influence over the lives of their church members. It is not uncommon for church leaders to have significant political and economic influence in their local communities. I spent time with an American doctor who had lived for many years in Africa. He was designing a huge development project that included building roads and opening businesses. His entire plan hinged

on getting church leaders involved so their members would be encouraged to become employees and customers. The involvement of church leaders would not ensure success, but their disapproval would absolutely cause failure.

Churches around the world are often the most influential distribution systems in their communities. Savvy governments and aid groups have long known this and use the influence of churches whenever feasible.

THE SECOND-BEST DISTRIBUTION SYSTEM

The second-best distribution system for poor people in the world is microfinance. Microfinance has already provided capital to over 500 million people, with billions more to come over the next twenty years. Why is microfinance such a good distribution system? Think about a typical SCA or MFI:

- Its members meet together at regular, often frequent, intervals.
- Its members exercise influence over one another.
- Its members come in contact with many nonmembers on a frequent basis.
- SCA or MFI leaders have a significant amount of actual and implied authority and credibility.
- If an SCA or MFI teams with a local church, it may benefit from some of the influence of that church.

Imagine a community bank meeting held at an open-air church building in the mosquito-infested jungles of Panama. The loan officer collects the weekly payments from sixteen borrowers, and then she introduces a nurse to talk about mosquito nets. The local preacher tells about another church twenty miles away where child deaths have decreased because the church members started using mosquito nets. The loan officer then informs the members that she has arranged for another nonprofit to distribute nets for free. She points out that mosquito nets have drastically reduced malaria among her other borrowers who use them regularly. Those influences alone should be enough to get the borrowers to act; however, microfinance makes adoption even more likely. Because of the cross guarantees, every borrower is at financial risk if other borrowers or their family members get malaria. Between the local pastor, a trusted loan officer, and the social demands of microfinance, there will be immense pressure to accept and use mosquito nets.

Community banking methodology also provides opportunities for the MFI to share values and beliefs and to mobilize borrowers toward a particular cause. Grameen Bank leveraged its reach to engage its clients in the political process in Bangladesh. Grameen Bank is committed to making sure all of its members and their families vote in every national election. In the 1996 election, 73 percent of the population turned out to vote, the highest percentage of voters ever recorded there. An indication that Grameen's efforts were effective was shown by the statistic that more women voted in that election than men, which was also another voting record. The following year, local elections were held at the village level. This time Grameen women not only voted but also became candidates. As a result of this social mobilization, more than two thousand Grameen members, many of them women, were elected into their local governing bodies.

Christian microfinance institutions have the ability to demonstrate and deliver the gospel message through the community bank model. In 2008, a research team visited a variety of clients in Rwanda and asked why they chose Urwego over competing MFIs. The answer was clear and consistent among randomly selected respondents: "Because we receive the Word of God!" Staff members of microfinance institutions are effective in sharing organizational "values and beliefs" that seem to be highly valued and prized by clients and in sharing the good news of Christ.

THE IMPORTANCE OF RELATIONSHIPS

Loan officers are the primary point of contact between borrowers and an MFI. These officers often become close friends and confidants of the borrowers they serve. If the loan officer is committed to sharing the gospel, many opportunities will occur to give a Bible, offer an invitation to a church service, or join a Bible study.

Rebecca is a loan officer for Esperanza in Los Alcorrizos, Dominican Republic. She works tirelessly to extend God's loving compassion to the poor. Her motivation flows from her former life — before being offered a position with Esperanza, she was a client who improved her own business after receiving some microloans. Rebecca still lives and works in the community in which she serves.

Having relationships with her clients is an important benefit of her position that Rebecca would never want to relinquish. She can recall many times her interactions with clients far exceeded the normal bounds of business — prayer for a family member in times of sickness, advice for pregnant teens, and visiting clients at their homes for holidays or other special occasions. She remembers one interaction that sits deep in her heart. During a visit to a client's home, Rebecca noticed the youngest child, age eighteen months, looked deathly ill from malnutrition. Wanting to help, Rebecca referred the child to a local clinic and, along with her church, raised the fees to enroll the child in a nutrition program. When asked how his life has changed since first interacting with Esperanza, the child's father, Manuel, says he is happy and has hopes and dreams for a better future in Christ. Through Rebecca's desire to go above and beyond her basic job, God's grace transformed hearts and lives.

DOUBLE WHAMMY

MFIs have an extra advantage *if* they can enlist the support of local churches because the churches may be able to provide distribution and acceptance advantages at little or no cost to the MFI. A good relationship would be beneficial for the local church and its members and the MFI. However, establishing a mutually beneficial relationship is not easy. As Brian Fikkert writes:[3]

> Many Christian MFIs have little vision for working with the local church, and those that do have such a vision have generally grown discouraged. MFIs often complain that churches can be bureaucratic, and their culture of grace has often made it difficult for their members to understand that loans are not grants and must be repaid. In addition, some churches' theological frameworks question MFIs' charging of interest and may even look down upon business and economic activity in general. Churches ... often state that MFIs are full of outsiders to the community who only care about business and about making money off of their parishioners.

Even though such partnerships are difficult, they are worth pursuing. Microfinance is a powerful method to help alleviate poverty without causing dependency, so it should be a natural tool for Christians to use. For many years, HOPE International has been the largest MFI in Ukraine. However, its other activity in Ukraine — growing children's clubs — is of greater interest to me and is a primary reason why I am a supporter of HOPE. These Tomorrow Clubs meet one day a week after school for about two hours. They are led by members of local churches who have been trained by HOPE employees. From the materials and guidelines written by HOPE, the children memorize Scripture, sing Christian songs, participate in local service projects, and play. Through these clubs, the children and their parents are encouraged to attend church or go to small group meetings. Additionally, the parents become aware of HOPE's microfinance activities that might be of benefit to them. By the fall of 2008, more than twelve thousand children in the Ukraine were attending these clubs every week.

MICROFINANCE PLUS

Helping poor people grow their incomes is, by itself, a worthwhile goal, yet there is so much more that can be done to improve their lives. If such services can be provided with little extra effort or cost, then why not do so? This is the vision of "microfinance plus": to provide a holistic range of services — insurance, counseling, training, immunizations, and so forth — to clients through the basic framework of microfinance. The distribution and acceptance potential of these other services makes microfinance attractive to a wide variety of nonprofit and for-profit organizations.

When an MFI decides to add a product or service to help its clients, it typically costs a small amount to do so. The MFI already has in place the necessary resources to make and collect microloans. It already has personnel who are respected and have an implied authority in their borrowers' lives. Because of this, many charities and nonprofit organizations are already working with MFIs, giving them products or services cheaply or at no cost because they know MFIs can distribute the products and help ensure their acceptance. The list of potentially helpful products and services that might improve the lives of the poor is limited only by imagination and need.

As members of the body of Christ, we believe the most important "product or service" that can be distributed to anyone is the gospel. How can the church partner with MFIs and SCAs to best address physical *and* spiritual needs? We will attempt to answer these questions in the following chapters as we explore microfinance more in depth.

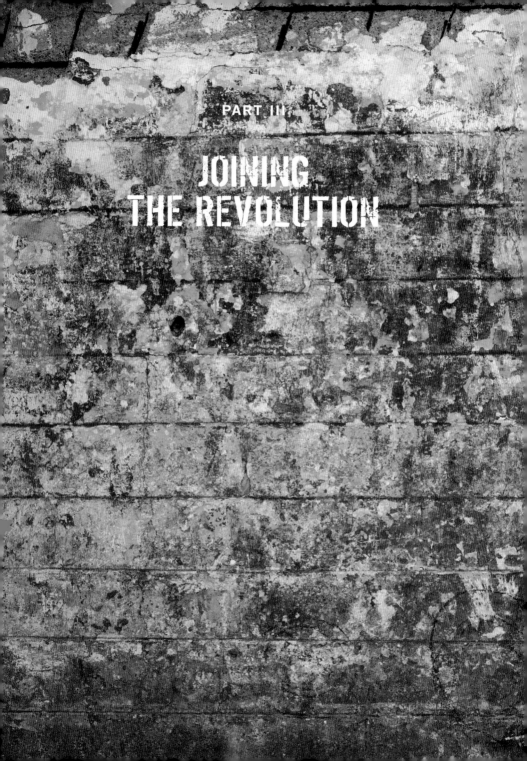

PART III

JOINING THE REVOLUTION

11

PASTORS SELDOM MAKE GOOD BANKERS

(PETER)

As we have seen, Savings and Credit Associations (SCAs) help the less fortunate improve their income, decrease their vulnerability, save for life-cycle events such as weddings and school fees, and increase their productivity. These benefits are magnified by church involvement, and it is important to look at how the local church can advance this powerful concept while fulfilling its other responsibilities.

Archbishop Emmanuel Kolini is the head of the Anglican Church in Rwanda and a leader within the worldwide Anglican movement. He founded the Anglican Mission in America, and a growing number of conservative congregations in the United States have chosen to be officially under his leadership.[1] In addition to his global influence, he continues to focus on the poor in his own country.

Kolini believes that SCAs are vital in carrying out the mandate of the church to alleviate both spiritual and physical poverty. When Kolini invited me to his humble office in Kigali, he explained his desire that every single congregation in the country would engage in this grassroots strategy: "If every church member could save $50 through SCAs, it would change their lives." Fifty dollars might be enough for me to pay part of my cell phone bill, but for many Rwandans, $50 is equivalent to a month's salary. It would be the first time these individuals had any sort of a safety net, and it would stimulate small-scale economic growth.

Kolini's vision may become reality. Since the Anglican Church began promoting SCAs in 2007, all dioceses have agreed to have at least three SCAs per church. It is expected that among the nearly two thousand congregations of the Anglican Church in Rwanda, a minimum of six thousand savings groups — averaging thirty members each — will be trained in saving, evangelism, and discipleship by 2010. Approximately 180,000 borrowers, nearly one million family members, will be touched by this initiative within one denomination in one small country in sub-Saharan Africa.

This model of mobilizing capital has enormous potential for replication and expansion to any region where local church leaders desire to help their congregations begin the journey out of poverty.

BENEFITS

Benefits to Churches: Service-Oriented Members. Church-based SCAs can help churches be recognized for their desire to serve and bring healing and wholeness to communities. This is particularly important in places where the image of the church suffers. Looking again at the Anglican Church's use of SCAs in post-genocide Rwanda, you can see this is critically important. During the 1994 genocide, about 800,000 individuals were murdered, many of them inside churches where they had fled for safety. There were a few priests, pastors, and church staff that either directly participated in the killings or stood by as their congregations were slaughtered en masse under church roofs and on church property. As a result, there were Rwandans who vowed never to return to church. In their eyes, the credibility of the church was destroyed. Thankfully, some of these strongly held views are beginning to soften as churches in Rwanda refocus on serving the community. With churches in Rwanda helping to organize SCAs, they are bringing one more element of healing and restoration in Rwanda.

Benefits to Individuals: Builds Relationships. God said it first: it is not good for man to be alone. This truth has echoed down through the millennia of human relationships. An Oromo proverb from Ethiopia agrees: *"Kophaan tchaala dansa"* or "Being alone is only good for going to the toilet."[2] For impoverished individuals, isolation makes an already difficult situation nearly impossible.

In the Bunyoro-Kitara Diocese of the Anglican Church of Uganda, an elderly woman faced an emergency operation and did not have the cash for the surgery. Her SCA met and resolved to assist her with 30,000 UGS ($18). The operation was successful and she gratefully explained that without the group's financial assistance, she would have died. SCAs are important for the poor and vulnerable because they develop and deepen relationships.

Listen to the following account of one church's SCAs:

The church we visited has three savings groups of thirty members each, all of which started as prayer groups. Some savings groups in Kigali use their savings to run a group business. This group comes once a week to the church and makes handicrafts for sale. A volunteer teacher from the church taught them to make these baskets. Seventeen of these women are living with HIV/AIDS and all of them have orphans who lost parents because of HIV/AIDS. They are using the group for support, extra income, and as an opportunity to pray.[3]

These women need each other for encouragement, prayer, and the training opportunities that the group provides.

Benefits to Individuals: Increases Income. In the Bunyoro-Kitara Diocese in Uganda, a church-based SCA is helping women take their very first economic steps. By mobilizing an incredibly small sum of money, women are able to start their own businesses and derive significant benefits from their increased income. One mother of four children took a $5.55 loan and made a local beverage which she sold in the local market. She used the profits to pay for her children's school fees. Another woman borrowed this same amount and bought fish at the lake and resold them in town. Another woman borrowed $11 to purchase a goat. And the list continues.[4] The impact of just a few dollars saved locally is amazing.

Benefits to International Agencies: Scale. Using SCAs with local churches allows rapid expansion within an existing infrastructure. In many parts of the world, churches are the only entity with such a wide reach. Brian Fikkert of the Chalmers Center describes his interaction with a group of women in the Masai tribe of Kenya who were participating in a church-based savings and credit association:

> Polygamy is the norm for these women, who are treated as second-class citizens ... [yet] these women were full of incredible joy as they held their heads high with dignity. For the first time in their lives these women understood that they were created in the image of God. As a result they were aggressively pursuing their own businesses and had a vision to serve as role models for other Masai women in even more remote areas.... As of November 2006, only 16 months into the project, there were already 232 savings and credit groups with 3,919 members, and rapid growth is continuing. [We] estimate that this ministry could conceivably reach a total of 20,000 members over five years.[5]

If the Chalmers Center did not partner with local churches, it would have been virtually inconceivable that they could have achieved such significant scale with the Masai in this same time period.

TRAINING THROUGH SCAs

Successful SCA programs often include lifestyle education. This training is critical for entrepreneurs who want to rise out of physical and spiritual poverty.

Mama Monique Ngalula lives in the Democratic Republic of the Congo, has nine children and fourteen grandchildren, and is committed to building a better world for her family. Mama Monique attended a training seminar on nutrition and recognized that the majority of the local beverage choices were extremely unhealthy and expensive. She saw not just a business opportunity but also an opportunity to improve the health of her community. She began producing nutritious juices and milk made from peanuts, soybeans, pinto beans, pomegranates, and other Congolese fruits.

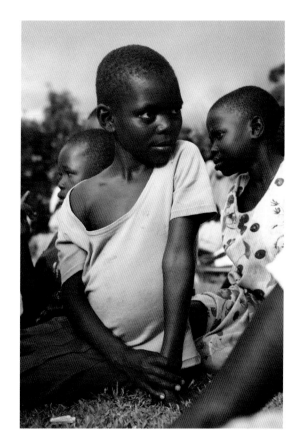

Mama Monique is more convinced than ever about the necessity of proper nutrition. She has since started a small group at her church to teach other women about nutrition and the importance of feeding children healthy meals. When asked about her dreams for the future, Mama Monique responded, "I want to see our children become healthier." She added, "I dream of opening a center in our community so that I can teach women and families about the value of nutritious meals." She is already teaching other women about health through local SCAs. The training in juice production and basic business principles Mama Monique received, coupled with a chance to access a lump sum of funding, significantly altered the physical poverty in her community.

Without the SCA infrastructure, it would have been difficult to provide training for Mama Monique, and the funding she required to start her juice business. SCAs are natural avenues to provide two key elements that break people out of poverty: training and capital.

CHANGED INCOME PLUS CHANGED HEARTS

SCAs naturally provide training that goes beyond technical issues. Church-based SCAs and microfinance initiatives emphasize biblical principles about responsibility, relationships, and service while pointing participants toward a loving Savior. This is critically important because, while increasing income is good, it does not automatically lead to a happier life.

After visiting entrepreneurs in the Philippines, Matt Krol, a board member of Youth With A Mission, observed that "money enables what's in a person's heart." He saw how some individuals seemed to pour their increased profits from their businesses into their families, communities, and churches, while others focused on using their increased capital for selfish purchases.

This is exactly why the church is uniquely qualified to engage in economic development. The church has the moral resources to transform hearts as it improves incomes. This combination is the only way that significant and lasting societal change is possible. Consider the contrasting examples of Florian and Milán.

Shortly after I arrived in Rwanda, I met Florian. He must have observed that I was looking at houses in the Kimihuhura neighborhood of Kigali, and he approached me and asked if he could be my guard and gardener. He explained that he lost his job and wanted to find a way of providing for his family. In Rwandan society, it is assumed that anyone with even a modest income will provide employment for a guard/gardener, and I was eager to do my part. Florian began working with me immediately. He taught me about the local plants and fruits, and I thought we had a friendship that was growing as quickly as the banana plants in the yard. After several months, however, I discovered that when I left, he was entering my house to steal money and valuables from my guests. Worse, he was using his wages and stolen funds for alcohol. I struggled to see how his increased income was

actually improving his life, and I recognized that unless Florian's heart was changed, no amount of extra money would make a difference.

The opposite was true for Milán Tapia, the Dominican entrepreneur mentioned in chapter 8, who turned her MFI-based financial success into educational opportunities for her community. Through her relationship with her loan officer, Milán came to know Jesus and wanted to use her income to make a difference in her community. With her business profits, she started a small school for the disadvantaged called *Tu Hogar Cristiano* (Your Christian Home). Her school began with a few students, but soon community members began bringing children to her, many from the streets. Milán became a teacher, mentor, and mother to these children, even as she continued to run her profitable business. By 2007, Tu Hogar Cristiano served roughly two hundred children each day, an amazing accomplishment considering Milán's humble beginnings. For Milán, increased income *along with* a changed heart resulted in an enormous amount of good for the community of San Pedro.

These contrasting examples show why the impact of SCAs and MFIs started in cooperation with a local church can be so much greater than SCAs and MFIs working alone. Lasting change can happen when hearts and wallets are transformed simultaneously.

GETTING INVOLVED

SCAs and MFIs are powerful because they provide individuals living in poverty a key tool with which to increase their income — access to a modest amount of capital. When combined with the local church, SCAs and MFIs can create lasting physical and spiritual change that flows out of the growing relationships between community members. American churches can promote SCAs and MFIs in ways that build the local church — often with only modest amounts of funding. Given these benefits, perhaps you are ready to learn more or even help implement an SCA.

The Chalmers Center for Economic Development (*www.chalmers.org*) provides resources for churches eager to get involved. Hosted by Covenant College, this center trains the church worldwide in how to minister to the poor without creating dependency. Its mission is "to help the church to help the poor to help themselves." The center advocates for churches to participate in advancing SCAs and to support microfinance. They provide distance learning courses, self-study material, and short-term classroom-based training institutes held throughout the world and hosted by local churches.

Whenever I am asked about ways for individuals to learn more about microenterprise development, my first response is to point people toward distance learning through the Chalmers Center. These online courses include guided reading programs and peer-to-peer interaction with other participants, normally from around the world.

Sarah Haig, who works for HOPE International based in Beijing, took these courses and commented, "The Chalmers Center courses were instrumental in guiding me to ask the right questions about poverty, justice, and my response as a believer, and then helping me develop the knowledge and tools to turn conviction into action. Chalmers' courses not only increased my technical capacity, but provided built-in accountability to use and apply what I'm learning for the furthering of my church, community, and the kingdom."

It is worthwhile to explore the geographic reach of organizations already experienced with SCAs. Consider the following:

- *Five Talents International* (*www.fivetalents.org*) is pioneering SCAs around the world with leaders of the Anglican Church. Five Talents was founded at the Lambeth Conference in 1998 and was charged with helping the Anglican Church create long-term solutions to poverty throughout the developing world. Five Talents helps the poor to fight poverty, create jobs, and transform lives through microfinance with a particular focus on SCAs.

- *LifeWind International* (*www.lifewind.org*) is a Christian organization that offers educational and technical support to microfinance projects. LifeWind hosts training seminars in related skills, including the establishment of SCAs, with the aim to make positive improvements in the living conditions of the poor. LifeWind works to help prevent disease, protect clean water sources, devise sanitation systems, and increase agricultural productivity, all through microenterprise development.

- As previously described, *HOPE International* (*www.hopeinternational.org*) was asked by the Anglican Church in Rwanda to help advance SCAs. As a result of this successful partnership, HOPE has expanded into India and the Democratic Republic of the Congo and is rapidly expanding this approach to addressing physical and spiritual poverty in other countries.

CHALLENGES

SCAs are poised to reach hundreds of thousands of additional entrepreneurs. SCAs are simple, yet effective. They avoid many of the problems associated with external involvement since their very design requires local ownership and participation. They require a fraction of the investment required to start a microfinance institution. They complement the activities of the local church and hold enormous promise to begin to put entrepreneurs on the pathway out of poverty. But they do not provide quick fixes or overnight successes.

The key question is whether the church in America will have the patience to promote and support a type of activity that results in foundational and incremental change. Or will the church migrate back to a system of handouts that provides immediate — but temporary — results. Our hope is that an increased focus on SCAs will be one indicator that the church is "in" for the long term and recognizes that some of the greatest impacts are seen over years, not days.

12

GETTING BEYOND
THE STARTING GATE

(PHIL)

Southern Hills Country Club is one of the truly great golf courses in America. Its elevated first tee overlooks a dogleg fairway and the skyline of downtown Tulsa. On a typical round, if one of the two traps on the right doesn't grab my ball, it's probably because I hit into the oak trees on the left. As I played a recent round with Tom Litteer — and as he stroked a 285-yard drive down the center of the fairway — he asked me, "Would you write one chapter for people like the ones in my church?"

We had been talking about the contents of this book, and Tom wanted to be able to recommend it to his parishioners in New Jersey. As we drove our cart down the hillside, he said, "You see, the people in my church are good-hearted, sincere Christians who want to show the love of Christ. But they are all pretty busy with their jobs and families. Could you write a chapter that just describes, step by step, how we might get involved in microfinance?"

Although that request sounded simple enough, I already knew some of the traps. I told some of my other friends, "Writing my first book was much simpler because religion was not involved. When you write to Christians, it's much more difficult to wade through theology, emotions, and beliefs." However, I believe Jesus would not have commanded us to share the gospel

in both word and deed unless there were practical ways to do it. So this chapter is for the folks in Tom's church and anyone else who wants to make a difference using microfinance but isn't sure how to get started.

CONSTRAINTS

The first step in choosing the best way to become involved with microfinance is to understand your own constraints, desires, and opportunities.

Through experience, I know that after learning about microfinance, many people and churches become enamored enough to want to start their own MFIs. As you consider that possibility, ask yourself several questions:

- *What human resources can I commit?* Operating a microfinance institution is as complicated as running a branch bank in America. That makes it beyond the scope of most churches or individuals. The complexity requires administrative know-how and an understanding of complex regulatory environments. Unless you have a substantial amount of human resources at your disposal, you are not likely to be able to start an MFI of any size.

- *What financial resources can I commit?* I often have people write for advice whose dreams and desires far outdistance their financial resources. Although these are not exact costs, the following may give you an idea of the high cost of providing microfinance: providing one microloan might cost $50 to $1,000; funding a village bank with an existing MFI might cost $5,000 to $25,000; funding for an existing MFI to move into a new country might cost $300,000 to $1 million; funding for the origination of an MFI might be $500,000 to $3 million.

- *What other resources can I commit?* God has provided us many resources and talents to use. For instance, you may not have any available financial resources, but you might be able to communicate with an MFI on a regular basis. Using this information, you might convince your small group to join you in regular prayer for the efforts of the MFI. Much more will be said about this in a later chapter.

- *What conflicts of interest might arise if my church has its own MFI?* Whenever I think about a church starting an MFI, I am reminded of something a microfinance professional once told me: "Christians do not always make good borrowers — they believe in grace, not works. If they don't pay back their loans, they expect complete forgiveness." As you start thinking about poor preachers handling large amounts of money or trying to collect loans from church members, it's easy to see the potential conflicts.

- *Will running an MFI be a bigger distraction than it's worth?* Again, an MFI is a complex operation. Other than very small projects, microfinance demands full-time, experienced professionals. Unless microfinance is the primary function of your organization, it may very possibly be a bigger distraction than it's worth.

- *Do I desire to make loans only to Christians?* In an effort to reduce the money commitment and to focus evangelical efforts, many Christians initially want to loan money only within the Christian community. This is very tricky for a variety of reasons. There might not be enough qualified borrowers in the Christian community; it might act as an inappropriate bribe for people to become Christians; and those who are disqualified from loans may be resentful. For those reasons, I almost never recommend that an MFI offer loans only to a particular group of Christians. I should point out, however, that this admonition does not apply to SCAs or even to MFI borrower groups who choose to self-limit themselves to other Christians.

Now that we have asked the questions to set the foundation, let's consider the basics of getting involved with microfinance using MFIs.

STEP BY STEP

There are many ways for Christians and churches to become involved with MFIs. Keeping the above questions in mind, here are some of the most likely possibilities:

- *Be an advocate.* To say I bombard my wife and friends with talk of microfinance is an understatement — maybe that's why I don't get invited to many parties. I love to talk about the benefits of microfinance and how it so cost effectively helps poor people and can be used to share the gospel. Over the past year I met many people who talk passionately about microfinance. These people serve as informal educators and are the reason why many faith-based organizations, civic organizations, nonprofits, and individuals have gotten involved with this life-changing concept. By telling fellow church members and missionaries about microfinance, you might help others involve their time, money, prayer, and energy in this worthy endeavor.

- *Make a donation.* A donation of virtually any size can help an existing MFI, especially if there are no strings attached. Although you might be able to earmark your donation for a particular country or project, it is unlikely that you can expect much input into the use of your donation unless it is quite large. One way donors who want to invest a modest amount can get involved is through Kiva at *kiva.org.* This organization allows people to make microloans to individuals in other countries through existing MFIs. The amounts needed are relatively small — investments start at $25 — so even children or youth groups can contribute. For the amount of money we typically spend on luxuries like unneeded Christmas presents, designer clothes, and eating out, we can make a practical difference in the life of an impoverished brother or sister. Although there is no link to Christianity through Kiva, it is a way for people to become acquainted with the concept of microfinance.

- *Fund a community bank.* Many MFIs would be pleased to have you or your church fund a community bank loan portfolio. All Souls Unitarian Church of Tulsa, Oklahoma, has funded thirty-two of FINCA International's community banks located in Nicaragua, Guatemala, Mexico, Haiti, Congo, and Kyrgyzstan. The members of All Souls have raised money through bake sales, dinners, youth group service projects, and holiday sales. All Souls not only asks its members to support these banks but endeavors to enlist the support of the wider community in Tulsa.

- *Fund a project.* There are some MFIs that hope to expand their projects beyond lending money. Fonkoze is an excellent MFI in Haiti, a country where over half of the population is illiterate. Fonkoze offers a literacy and life-skills educational program to its borrowers. Although literacy is not a requirement for the first loan, by the time a borrower has a third loan, she must be enrolled in one of Fonkoze's 250 literacy centers located around the island. Funding this program, especially for the very poorest, is a strain on Fonkoze's operational budget. This type of specific project — and projects like pastoral training, nutrition education, and job training — is the kind that donors or sponsors could choose to fund for specific impact.

- *Loan to an MFI.* Many people are choosing to loan money to MFIs at low interest rates so that the money can be put to work helping poor people while, at the same time, making a small profit for the lenders. Loans can be made either directly to institutions or through funds which diversify among many MFIs.

As a businessperson, I understand that many MFIs will choose to increase their lending base by taking loans themselves. However, being in debt obviously increases the risk of the MFI not surviving hard times and increases the risk to anyone loaning to the MFI. Some

MFIs borrow up to ten times as much as they have in equity. If those MFIs do not survive, it harms their lenders and the poor people to whom the MFIs have made microloans. MFIs that portray themselves as Christian take on the additional obligation of repayment because it is the biblical thing to do. If they choose to borrow, they should take special care not to borrow too much so that they do not compromise the cause of Jesus.

- *Bring microfinance to a new country via an existing MFI.* Some folks at my church wanted to start a large microfinance project in Volgodonsk, Russia. We raised $500,000, but we didn't want to start our own MFI. Instead, we partnered with HOPE International to administer the MFI in Russia. HOPE's experience in the nearby region of Ukraine allowed it to design and run the program with comparative ease. HOPE also has the desire to share the gospel, so it made a natural partnership. HOPE's expertise has kept the project on track, and it has become a self-sufficient microfinance institution in Russia that will benefit thousands of entrepreneurs.

When Mars Hill Bible Church in Grandville, Michigan, considered international engagement, they partnered with Turame, World Relief's microfinance institution in Burundi. This partnership is regularly featured in Mars Hill's materials, website, and sermons. Willowdale Chapel in Kennett Square, Pennsylvania, took a similar approach when partnering with HOPE in the Masina commune of Kinshasa in the Democratic Republic of the Congo.

In these examples, both the implementing organizations and the churches in the United States have learned valuable lessons about what makes a successful partnership. Don Golden, former executive pastor at Mars Hill and now senior vice president of church engagement at World Relief, described the changing face of partnership this way: "The history of dominance among parachurch agencies calls for a special willingness to relinquish control and to foster a shared mission agenda." Gone are the days of passive partnerships. Instead, both implementers and churches are ready for a "live" relationship, marked by:

Limited Focus to One Geographic Area. Both Mars Hill and Willowdale Chapel recognized that by focusing their efforts on one particular area it would be possible to increase the "ownership" their church body feels. You might like having more dots on your "map" of places that you're serving, but focusing on one area allows you to actually know the people you're partnering with. Long-term relationships matter. Arguably, three trips to the same place to develop relationships make a more significant impact than three trips to different places.

Information Flow. It is far better to overcommunicate in these partnerships. Without regular contact with church members, partnerships grow cold. Regularly scheduled bulletin inserts, pictures on slides, videos, and hearing directly from practitioners are each

critical. During a church service at Willowdale, the pastor made a telephone call to the managing director in Congo so his congregation could hear an update.

Visits. Despite advances in communication technology, there is still no substitute for face-to-face interaction. Annual trips by a few key members of a congregation help keep foreign partnerships immediate. Additionally, church members with specific skills can bring insight and training to the in-country staff. Jim Krimmel is a professor at Messiah College, a certified public accountant, and a certified fraud examiner. Krimmel traveled to the Philippines, Congo, and Ukraine with HOPE International, leading fraud prevention training and conducting assessments on the internal controls over loan disbursements and repayments.

Engagement by Church Members. Qualified and interested members, interns, or staff members are key in developing relationships with an MFI. There are certainly ways to connect individuals who are gifted in finance, marketing, and writing to the organization's needs in short-term and longer-term service opportunities, as will be discussed later.

CHOOSING A MICROFINANCE ORGANIZATION

To finish our step-by-step instruction in how to become involved in microfinance, here are some suggestions about choosing a particular MFI as a partner. There are thousands of microfinance organizations, so the following represents a synthesis of what I typically recommend.

The process starts with finding out which constraints mentioned in the first part of this chapter are most important. Depending on the answers, other questions will follow. Does the project need to be done in a specific community or country? Is a particular type of project required in addition to the microfinance, such as clean water or AIDS education? Must the project be overtly Christian?

If somebody wants to invest in microfinance or if the project is to be done in a specific community or country, I recommend going to the website for The Mix Market, *www.mixmarket.org*. Go to Mix Market Profiles to view important statistics for over a hundred microfinance investment funds and 1,300 MFIs. By reviewing the websites of the various organizations, you can usually narrow your choices down to a few organizations.

In the event that you want to deal with a large multinational MFI network, some of the ones you might consider are ACCION International, FINCA International, HOPE International, Opportunity International, and Pro Mujer. There are other multinational aid organizations which also engage in microfinance, including World Concern, World Relief, and World Vision.

The number of microfinance organizations consistently and clearly concerned with overtly promoting Christianity is small. Of these, many are MFIs that work in only one country and can best be found through The Mix Market as pointed out above. If you want to deal with an MFI that overtly promotes Christianity, take the time to review their annual reports, websites, and advertising, and then talk to several people who work there. Make sure they truly promote Christianity in a way you desire.

MICROFINANCE AND RELATIONSHIPS

Microfinance is about more than providing loans and financial services. The most powerful aspect of microfinance as it relates to Christianity may be its ability to form lasting, deep relationships, typically involving the borrower and the MFI's loan officer. Such relationships are important opportunities for evangelism, both formal and informal.

Wang lives in China and provides for her grandparents and mother-in-law. After thirteen microloans, she has developed her music store from a ten-square-foot stall that sold guitars into a sixty-square-foot store selling ten different types of instruments and offering music lessons. Through the witness and friendship of her loan officer, Wang became a Christian and began attending church regularly. She said, "We became good friends and communicated about family and faith. My loan officer was a great help to me in my spiritual walk." In addition to improving her spiritual walk and sharing her faith, Wang wants to continue growing her store and manage a music conservatory.

The business environment is where people spend much of their waking time, develop friendships, and gain the respect of their peers. It would have been difficult to initially invite Wang to church, but it was easy for the loan officer to develop a business relationship in which Christ was modeled and shared.

Participation in a microfinance venture can sometimes be daunting, but the rewards are significant. Becoming involved with microfinance is much more rewarding than playing a few rounds of golf, even at Southern Hills. So, Tom, don't let your parishioners stay uninvolved just because they are busy. However, as they become involved, they should be aware of a number of pitfalls awaiting Christian microfinance efforts that they need to avoid.

13

KEEPING OUR EYES
ON THE PRIZE

(PETER)

A pastor in Rwanda told me that he had tried to launch a microfinance program several years earlier. With a rueful chuckle, he described how disastrous it was and how he lost two things.

> First, I lost money as people assumed that money coming from the church was a grant, not a loan. Second, I lost people in my church. If individuals were late on payments, they would not come to church. Perhaps they were nervous that I'd ask for their repayment as they were leaving the church, or that I'd preach a difficult message targeted right at them. It just didn't work.

This pastor recognized that it is possible to harm the church while trying to do acts of service. Inappropriately organized or administered microfinance supports the Swahili proverb *"Kiaribucho urafiki ni kukopa na kuazima"* — "that which spoils friendship is borrowing and lending."[1]

From personal experience, I know that if the design of a microfinance project is wrong, there will be virtually no end to the difficulties. Relationships will be strained and ministries will be harmed. The tools described in this book could have a negative effect if used improperly. It is our hope that we can save you some of the tears many others have already shed.

This chapter highlights several important cautions that will help ensure success when implementing microfinance. It is divided into two sections: operational issues and specific challenges for the church.

OPERATING WITH EXCELLENCE

When creating or managing a microfinance institution, there are internal operational issues that significantly influence the likelihood of running a successful program.

INTERNAL CONTROLS

Nothing hurts the ministry of a church more than moral failure. I have heard of several Westerners who wanted to support local entrepreneurs by giving funds to local churches, expecting the money would be used properly. "We trust the local pastors and entrepreneurs — we know they have good hearts." This is a common sentiment, yet we could actually be placing our brothers and sisters in compromising situations.

It would be beyond foolish to encourage a pastor, while on the road, to share a hotel room with a single person of the opposite sex, or for a pastor to take up the offering every Sunday without any oversight. Who would willingly place a leader in these tempting situations? Yet simply handing large amounts of money to our brothers and sisters overseas, relying exclusively on trust, is often setting them up to fail, both financially and morally. If we are serious about assisting, we do them a greater service by first installing strong systems of internal controls and accountability.

Although the amounts of money involved in microfinance might be small compared to American standards, they easily amount to *years* of wages for any one person in Bangladesh or Malawi or Peru. It is not fair to tempt church leaders with these amounts of money when their families may be faced with immediate financial needs. Imagine a local pastor who receives a large sum of money to be used in microfinance on the same day he learns his daughter needs an expensive surgical procedure. Local church leaders and pillars within the Christian community have brought shame to the church's mission — sometimes with good intentions and sometimes maliciously — that could have been prevented with rigorous controls to minimize temptation and ensure that funds are used according to their intended purpose.

COUNT THE COST

A woman who had served as a lifelong missionary in Africa inherited $10,000. With excitement in her voice, she described how she had heard of microfinance and that she was interested in having our organization begin a new microfinance institution in the community where she had served. I didn't want to dampen her excitement, but the reality is that $10,000 is not sufficient capital to create a microfinance institution.

This woman is not alone. Starting a full-fledged microfinance institution is an extremely costly venture. You need appropriate computer systems that can track repayments and loan officer performance. You need enough capital to support an administrative office. Doing quality microfinance normally requires a seven-digit amount of money per country — and you can't count past the decimal point!

THE RIGHT SKILLS

Many people and organizations now starting microfinance programs have been focused on traditional charity and missions. However, microfinance requires a different skill set. If you haven't balanced your checkbook recently, it's likely you aren't the right person to lead a new business venture.

SUSTAINABILITY AND INTEREST RATES

One of the most powerful aspects of microfinance is that it can cover its operating costs. This allows an entity to operate over many years or even decades. Achieving this goal requires an interest rate sufficient to cover local operating costs. There are too many examples of MFIs that have fizzled out due to insufficient revenue, leaving loan recipients in exactly the same position they were in before. The entrepreneurs most MFIs serve are looking for long-term savings and credit, not another short-term project that will end.

SERIOUS ABOUT REPAYMENTS

Since we're focused on helping people who are desperately poor, shouldn't we just forgive the few borrowers who might not be able to pay back a loan? Surely we don't need the money as much as they do, right? This common sentiment will not only cause repayment rates to plummet, but it also has the potential to hurt the area in the long term as local individuals will be conditioned not to repay. Once the "credit well" is poisoned, it is difficult for other groups to operate in the area. If entrepreneurs did not repay the last microfinance institution, they have an assumption that the word "credit" is really just a disguised grant. And when grants are mixed with loans, all you get are groans!

WORK WITH THE GOVERNMENT

Governments get squeamish when outsiders enter their country to lend money. And for good reason. There are too many examples of unscrupulous behavior in the lending industry, even in the developed world, for regulators to turn a blind eye. They know that lack of trust in financial institutions sends shock waves throughout an economy. Those lending money and engaging in savings must do so in a way that builds the financial infrastructure of a country. They need to cooperate with laws and requirements of local officials in good faith and to the best of their ability.

KEEPING THE MISSION

While these issues are common to anyone engaged in microfinance, the following challenges are specific to churches engaged in this form of poverty alleviation.

AVOID RICE CHRISTIANITY

When some of the first English missionaries to Asia confronted the region's grinding poverty some two hundred years ago, they saw the people's dire need for rice and gave away all the rice they could. They persuaded

Christians in England to donate money for rice, which they purchased locally and distributed to the needy. The missionaries were sincere and well-meaning, and as long as they provided rice, the locals attended church — the size of services increased substantially. But when the rice ran out, the churches emptied. These church folk became known as "Rice Christians."

Good works, like offerings of rice or capital, are a critical part of serving Jesus Christ, but when they are used in a way that rewards religious involvement, the resulting faith of the followers is most likely shallow or nonexistent. When the church engages in microfinance, it can appear that an organization is bribing people into the kingdom of God. This is not the biblical understanding of service. Unfortunately, even when the church doesn't intend to do this, others can still misunderstand the church's motivation. This is one reason why we encourage microfinance institutions to love and serve all with equal treatment and not to have partiality for entrepreneurs from local churches.

KEEP THE MISSION CENTRAL

Healthy organizations grow and develop. Unwillingness to adapt to changing circumstances is a recipe for stagnancy and irrelevance. Yet an organization can adapt so much that there is nothing left of the original. Many organizations founded on Christ have adapted their mission and practice in ways that make them unrecognizable when compared to their original mission.

Consider Barclay's Bank. Its original mission statement was "To create honorable employment and beneficial businesses that honor God." Founding documents describe how each day was to begin with prayer, and faith was to be infused into every aspect of the bank's operations.[2] Looking at Barclay's today, it is difficult to find evidence of these religious roots or founding practices. Why did the bank drift so far from its founding mission? Is it bad when a faith-based bank or microfinance institution drifts from the faith component of its work?

After hearing a presentation on HOPE International, several executives from a leading nonprofit organization that builds homes expressed their surprise at how overt we are about our faith and asked, "Aren't you worried that you will offend some people?" I later learned that less than fifteen years ago, their organization was open about faith. But this candle was snuffed out after they discovered individuals outside the organization did not approve of anything "religious" in their work. To accommodate a wider audience — and secure more funding — they slowly buried their original motivation and methodology.

To protect against a gradual mission drift requires an intentional approach that connects the actions and practices of an organization to its mission. At HOPE, ensuring that we have an impact on physical and spiritual poverty is at the core of our identity. The focus on spiritual poverty is the only hope for lasting transformation for the poor. To protect this spiritual focus, we highlight spiritual development in every single internal newsletter, we focus on discipleship during staff retreats, we routinely monitor our progress on key spiritual metrics, and, most importantly, we are committed to hiring people with not only the right skills but the right hearts for ministry — people described as having the head of a businessperson but the heart of a pastor.

PARTNER WITH THE LOCAL CHURCH

Which do you think has a greater chance of spreading throughout the developing world and surviving for years to come: local churches or foreign microfinance institutions? The church has been present for hundreds and even thousands of years, and most would agree that it will outlast any other institution, including self-sufficient microfinance institutions. As a result, it makes sense to include the local church in our poverty alleviation efforts. The local church has the mandate and mission to remain active locally.

The Anglican archbishop of Rwanda, Emmanuel Kolini, described an experience he had with a prominent Christian relief and development or-

ganization engaged in microfinance. "When they arrived in Rwanda, they asked us for our help. We helped them register, find the right connections, and set up their operations. Yet as soon as things were moving, they turned their back on the local church."

Ignoring the local church is not an option for organizations devoted to Christ. Not only will the local church outlast foreign organizations, but the local church is often the most influential institution in a community. It would be a waste not to use the most obvious and beneficial resource available. Further, for long-term benefits for the kingdom, it is imperative to grow local church leadership and improve the lives of members. They are God's heart and hands in those communities, and we need to work closely with them as part of the same body.

In China, HOPE pioneered microfinance in some remote regions north of Beijing. The HOPE country director had a passion for the unreached people and was pushing the frontier on microfinance. A survey of all loan recipients in one branch discovered that more than half of the clients said they heard about Jesus Christ for the very first time through HOPE. Individuals were seeing the benefit of microfinance and hearing about the love of Jesus Christ — and they were responding.

Unfortunately, the local church was simply nonexistent, and these individuals were left without access to further spiritual development. In an area where freedom of religion is severely restricted by the government, there were few options. HOPE did not have the ability or expertise to launch churches or disciple clients to become fully devoted followers of Christ. HOPE had helped spread the gospel and introduced many to Jesus Christ but was unable to see these new Christians grow in maturity.

Young Christians need spiritual guidance, so we now focus on working in areas that have a local church presence or partner with a church-planting ministry. This allows us to ensure that newly believing clients can become part of healthy churches.

MEASURE AND COMPARE RESULTS

A 2004 survey tracked funding released by the Ministry of Finance in Chad that was intended for rural health clinics. The survey's goal was to determine how much of the funding actually reached the clinics. It was not concerned with whether the clinics spent it well or even if it made a positive impact on the community, only with whether it arrived. The findings were shocking. Research concluded that "less than 1 percent of [the funding] reached the clinics — 99 percent failed to reach its destination."[3] Where was the accountability?

Accountability is a bedrock principle in the business world, where the clear bottom line of profit makes it possible to assess performance. However, nonprofit organizations often have little accountability and few techniques with which to allocate more resources to the most effective programs. Nonprofits — and for-profit MFIs — must decide what to monitor and how to monitor it in order to ensure performance.

Measuring performance indicators like the total amount of money loaned, repayment rates, and return on equity are necessary to build a high-performing MFI. Measuring impact in the realm of Christ-centered microfinance is much more difficult. Along with the provision of loans, how do we know if individuals are becoming less hostile to the claims of Jesus or growing in their faith? Unfortunately, "the quality of fund-raising literature ... seems to matter far more than the quality of work."[4] There is virtually no oversight of what organizations do: "They are continents away from the people who've entrusted them with their cash."[5]

Despite the difficulty, there needs to be accountability — we *all* need it! For example, in addition to external audits and agency ratings, HOPE International hired a director of spiritual integration to help assess the spiritual impact of our microfinance efforts. He coordinates with local leadership to ensure that each country is monitoring and measuring culturally appropriate activities and results. This tracking includes everything from the impact on local church tithing to the number of times the gospel is presented. We believe this monitoring will help guide and ensure a holistic impact on the lives of clients.

THE POOR DON'T LIKE BEING POOR

As you engage in microfinance and begin helping individuals work their way out of poverty, you might encounter people who question whether escaping poverty is really a good thing. Greg Mortenson, author of *Three Cups of Tea*, experienced such sentiments to his work in Korphe, a village tucked away in the Karakoram Mountains in Pakistan. He noted that Westerners tend to romanticize poverty. "Many Westerners passing through the Karakoram had the feeling that the Balti lived a simpler, better life than they did back home in their developed countries." Many within the church have a tendency to do the same. Aren't the poor closer to God? Isn't that a blessing?

Mortenson noticed that this "paradise" of the simpler and better life existed only in fantasy. The reality: "In every home, at least one family member suffered from goiters or cataracts. The children, whose ginger hair he had admired, owed their coloring to a form of malnutrition called kwashiorkor … the nearest doctor was a week's walk away in Skardu, and one out of every three Korphe children died before reaching their first birthday."

As we work to help the poor, we need to be careful of the dangerous romanticism that can sneak into our perspective. The poor do *not* like living in poverty, and nearly every poor person, when given an opportunity, is eager to work toward a better material life. There is a world of difference between the voluntary poverty of someone like Mother Teresa and the abject involuntary poverty that hurts billions of people around the world.

Given the significant challenges inherent in operating a successful microfinance institution, many organizations see partnerships as an attractive option. Specifically, churches that partner with microfinance institutions become voices that are critical in protecting the organization's mission. But to engage in these partnerships, we must ask whether the church has any business doing business in the first place.

14

GOD'S BUSINESS

(PHIL)

My welcome to the world of high finance happened on a cold winter day in Minneapolis, Minnesota. I was making a presentation for our company's second public offering to one of America's best known mutual fund managers. Our underwriters assured us that if we sold this guy, the "deal was done." That comment was all the more reason for me to be nervous when the manager asked to have a private one-on-one meeting with me. Although highly irregular, the underwriters decided to give in to the request.

Sitting down at an antique pinewood table, the manager grabbed a walnut, stared at me with cold, clear eyes, and said, "Go." For the next twenty-two minutes I stared back in his eyes and gave the complex presentation from memory while he bounced the walnut on the table about every ten seconds.

After 132 walnut bounces and no eye blinks, he said only, "I buy stocks based on my evaluation of management. I think you are honest. Are you capable of following your business plan?" After I answered with a stark "Yes," he ushered me out of the conference room and all of us out of his building.

As I sat shell-shocked in the back of the limousine and tried to explain

the surreal meeting to the underwriters, they got a phone call saying the fund manager would take 10 percent of the deal. As the underwriters had promised, other fund managers followed his lead, and the deal was done when, a few days later, our company completed the offering. The fund manager was willing to rely on me if I could convince him that I was capable of actually doing what I said I would do (and later did).

Unfortunately, many around the world do not believe Christians and the church successfully meet this requirement as it concerns sharing the gospel with the whole world. Businesspeople in particular are often skeptical. This is a tragedy. Fulfilling the mission to effectively alleviate physical and spiritual poverty requires the business community to become involved. And by "involved" I do not mean only funding some project. As one business leader cynically decried, "The only time I hear from my pastor is when there is a capital campaign and they need my money."

More astute church leaders understand that business and the church can be great partners. One exceptionally perceptive church leader wrote, "The promotion of productive economic activity contributes to the growth of the church, and to the presentation of a holistic Gospel that includes 'doing good.' It also presents concepts that the church can use to generate income to sustain its own ministries, even to the extent of funding international mission outreach."[1] I agree. Using the tool of business, the church has an excellent opportunity to integrate physical and spiritual missions.

EMPLOYMENT-BASED SOLUTIONS

Microfinance, using SCAs and MFIs, is one type of an employment-based solution. Peter and I especially like microfinance because it is so cost efficient, can be replicated to help hundred of millions of people, is useful to combine with other services, and is an excellent tool to help spread the good news.

In the next two chapters we will examine other types of employment-based solutions that are useful in situations where Christians want to help in specific geographic locations or with certain types of groups. Some of these solutions are especially useful where an individual has special talents to share or where God has called churches or people to work in locations that are difficult to access.

A problem the church has around the world is how to share the good news in "closed countries." These countries prohibit the entry of missionaries or individuals whose primary purpose is sharing the gospel. Some of the prohibitions occur by strict laws, while others occur by limiting visas. Employment-based solutions are often the best way to gain entry into these countries. Without naming names, I know of many countries which are highly repressed on political or social grounds but have allowed in organizations and individuals bringing employment-based solutions. Although there may be limits placed on the extent to which the gospel can be verbally shared, there are few limits on modeling a Christlike lifestyle.

THE POTENTIAL ROLE OF BUSINESS IN ENTREPRENEURSHIP

Churches and ministries never have sufficient time, talent, and money to accomplish all they wish. However, additional resources already exist in the form of businesspeople within the church who are an essential and underutilized part of fighting physical and spiritual poverty. You can see one of the most obvious reasons business is important if you glance at your calendar, especially if it looks somewhat like mine.

The past week was typical. I went to church at 8:00 a.m. on Sunday. Counting the other times I go to church for other services or youth group activities, I might average five hours a week in the building. Even though I suspect that amount of time is above the national average, it pales in comparison to the forty to fifty hours a week most people spend in business settings. Even counting the time spent in small groups, the simple fact is that, for most of us, we spend far more time developing relationships and interacting with those in the world of work than we do in the world of church.

The church I attend demonstrates another advantage of involving businesspeople in the mission of alleviating spiritual and physical poverty. On a typical Sunday, we have over a thousand Christians enter our doors. That is certainly something to celebrate. But we seldom have many non-Christians pop in for a visit and, despite our best efforts, many of those infrequent visitors find it difficult to follow the terminology or get meaningfully engaged. Business offers an environment where non-Christians can watch the behavior of committed Christians and learn about Christianity at their own pace and in their own way. Business is a window through which the people who most need the gospel can watch Christ at work in the everyday lives of Christians.

Leonard Shoultz is the most organized and thorough man I know. He sends out multiple emails ahead of any meeting to make sure everybody possible attends. As an additional enticement, he even details the treats that will be available. He once asked me for information about SCAs, and I sent him several massive documents about the subject. I suspected he would quickly scan the hundreds of pages like I did, but later found out he had closely read every single page. This retired whirlwind is now providing the skills needed to organize a missionary effort to a politically repressed country. Leonard is not organized just because God gave him the gift of organization. Rather, he took the abilities God gave him and sharpened them through his education and employment. Business prepared him to help in the mission field. I can't even imagine the number of people in the business world who were influenced by his Christian witness as it was demonstrated every day. Leonard reminds me of another businessman who became a king.

David ben Jesse was in charge of a few scraggly sheep that he chased around the desert. Even so, his job taught him the necessary skills to challenge and defeat the most feared warrior of his era, manage hundreds of the worst employees imaginable while hiding from the law, and amass possibly the largest fortune ever in

silver and gold. His business experience was a positive influence as David, his sons, and employees wrote some of the most loved parts of the Bible. God thought his story was so good that there is more written about David in the Old Testament than about any other person. Pretty impressive for a blue-collar worker with no formal church training.

Business is one of the best places to develop trustworthiness and competence. It teaches strategic planning and execution. Business leaders within the church are capable of discovering creative solutions to stubborn problems and helping keep the church on mission.

One Christian leader busy unlocking the potential of businesspeople is Bob Roberts Jr., the pastor of NorthWood Church in the Dallas and

Fort Worth area. He and his church members are fully committed to business-centric missions and discipleship. They have planted more than eighty-nine churches in the U.S. and are focused on carrying out the Great Commission in the world. They realize the central role the business community must play in this process. Bob writes about the example of the early church in this process. "When people saw Christianity within the context of community, farmers and workers and maidservants living a transformed life, *their witness* transformed the larger system and society ... Programs did not carry the enthusiasm of the gospel in the early church. People did."[2]

He continues, "In our present-day congregation in Texas, we have a growing number of businesspeople, lawyers, doctors, and the like who are all going into the ministry in our church ... We encourage them to use their jobs, not leave their jobs, because their job is their venue into the very mission field they love. This is the living example of the early church."

Terry Deckard exemplifies the many people who have taken another step and followed their calling to help others full time rather than make more money. "A divorce spurred her to move up the corporate ladder from part-time bookkeeper in the early 1980s to certified public accountant and managing partner in the accounting firm Gainer, Donnelly & Desroches. Twenty years later, a mission trip to Africa prompted Deckard to sell off her stake in that partnership, leave the corporate world, and raise money to fund micro-businesses in the African nations of Malawi, Kenya, and Zimbabwe." Her organization, Exodus Force Initiative, works to break the cycles of poverty and famine by building sustainable local economies. She says, "We work to set up chicken and vegetable farms with water wells for irrigation so people can plant all year whether it rains or not. A lot of the time this is the only clean water around. The alternative for these people is often walking a couple of miles to the river, and even then, the water isn't good."[3] Many villages have profited from Deckard's business background where she learned to analyze problems, find innovative solutions, raise needed money, and manage projects to a successful conclusion.

A NEW DEFINITION OF RETIREMENT

The amount of wealth generated in the United States in the last hundred years is staggering. Many who are rich in resources are choosing to invest their time and money in helping the church serve the poor and share Christ. However, this is not the only trajectory a successful businessperson can take. If the church does not act in a meaningful way to involve these people in God's vision and mission, many will probably be lost by the wayside, like I nearly was.

I retired at age fifty, moved to a new community, played golf nearly every day, and was close to becoming addicted to a pleasurable, self-centered lifestyle. Fortunately, I was shocked into reality by a conversation at a Christmas party. A wealthy man who made his fortune selling kitchen countertops complained to me that his friends didn't understand his plight. "You know how it is," he said to me, "up in the morning, breakfast, golf, lunch, nap, dinner with friends, and then the same thing the next day — it's *so* tiring and boring."

It shames me to admit that I *did* understand what he meant. How had I reached a place where I could think and feel such a thing? Fortunately, God-ordained circumstances soon conspired to change my life. Otherwise, I would likely still be pouring my time, energy, and money into earthly treasures with no lasting value.

Retired and soon-to-be-retired people have a special potential to change the world. These people have the knowledge, contacts, time, and resources to make a tremendous impact in solving some of the world's most difficult problems. Already there are many organizations taking special advantage of this group. One organization, Halftime, helps businesspeople transition from successful careers to significant "retirements" — if you can call the excitement and wonder involved in serving God and others "retirement."

The founder of Halftime, Bob Buford, exemplifies what it means to change from a life of financial success to one of eternal significance. Bob sold his East Texas cable television company and embarked on the entirely unrelated career of equipping and encouraging people to lead exciting and fulfilling second careers in serving other people. In addition to writing several books and founding Halftime, Bob and his friends started Leadership Network to help equip innovative Christian leaders. The organization endeavors to help churches grow quickly by developing communities where leaders share information about their growth successes and failures, and jointly commit to high-growth strategies. Leadership Network has had a dramatic impact on hundreds of churches.

My friends John and Penny Alden represent a different type of "retiree." John was a nurse midwife and Penny had spent nineteen years homeschooling their four children. They lived in the small town of Okmulgee, Oklahoma, when they understood that God was calling them to Honduras. As Penny refreshed her latent skills as a registered nurse and John began to wind down his first career, they immersed themselves in learning Spanish. Now they work as nurses at Loma de Luz hospital on the edge of the jungle on the north shore of Honduras. Through their interactions in the hospital and involvement in surrounding communities, they have helped teach and encourage many people, not only how to care for their bodies but also how to care for their souls. From the first, they worked with a small church plant and recently had the pleasure of dedicating a new church building which the members mostly constructed themselves with funding from America. John and Penny continue to work and worship with these people, believing that they will see the greatest harvest for the kingdom with a passionate investment in the lives of the people they touch daily.

Some people take their talents and business skills to other countries to build large, long-lasting organizations. Predisan began in 1986 when the family of Robert Clark moved from Atlanta, Georgia, to Honduras. Their goal was to teach basic health care principles and techniques to community health volunteers. Almost from the beginning, their work was overseen and sponsored by the Northlake Church of Christ in Atlanta.

Although Robert Clark died in 1994, his wife, Doris, continued the work. The leadership of Predisan made significant efforts to instill their mission and passion to other personnel so there would be no significant mission drift. Amanda Madrid has consulted with Predisan for more than twenty years. She and Doris Clark have mentored a long-time employee, Martha Rivera, who is now the executive director. Predisan has flourished through the years. In 2006 it had seventy full-time Honduran employees, including three physicians, one dentist, and two psychologists. That year it provided educational services and medical care in more than 42,000 instances to thousands of different people and brought spiritual teaching and hope through the work of its chaplains, the staff, and activities with a spiritual component.[4]

INTERNATIONAL EXPERTISE IS VITAL

One of my friends works with a remote community in the African country of Uganda. The locals manufacture a craft item that he believes would sell well in America. However, he doesn't know how the community can develop a marketing and sales relationship with an American firm — which probably doesn't matter since they have no cost-effective method of shipping their products. Even that probably doesn't matter, since there is no financing method available to move money back and forth between America and this community. My friend cares about this community, but he needs to partner with innovative businesspeople who can overcome daunting obstacles. Without my friend's concern and commitment, it is possible that no one in the West would care — or even know — about this tiny community. Without help from business professionals, my friend's concern may not translate into tangible results for his community.

American businesses are already familiar with overcoming obstacles in every country in the world. One of the businesses in which I have invested is relatively tiny, yet it has dealings in many developing countries. Its

sales and accounting staffs have established relationships with countless people internationally and understand how to get things done in countries like Nigeria, Saudi Arabia, and Indonesia. Sharing the gospel and helping people would be less difficult than the tasks they already accomplish. Just think of the skills being acquired by Christians already working for international giants like GE and Coca-Cola.

A seldom acknowledged fact is that there are already indigenous Christian businesspeople in virtually every country of the world. While it might take outsiders a long time to establish relationships and trust, these men and women hold the potential to quickly make an impact for the kingdom of God in developing countries. Frederick S. Mulalira Kawuma is the managing director of ACLAIM Africa Limited, a management consultancy firm based in Kampala, Uganda. He said, "Corruption in the workplace is a major challenge in Uganda. As you talk to people you realize that some want to use influence (money) to get a job or a contract. Another challenge is the poor skills and lack of professionalism in the marketplace." To solve such problems, he and his company focus on leadership development and promote a high standard of morality and ethical behavior. Kawuma believes that he represents Christ in the work environment and shares his love through his work.[5]

The church in the United States has the potential to unleash an army of servants to every corner of the globe. Tens of millions of baby boomers are preparing to leave the business world over the next decade. Many, if not most, are relatively healthy and wealthy — imagine if they use their resources to expand and deepen the kingdom of God in developing countries!

In addition, many members of younger generations understand that working for social and economic justice is more important than simply making money. Followers of Jesus Christ in the business community are already modeling the gospel in their work environments. Together, these highly skilled businesspeople from the church — from all countries and of all ages — have the resources to change the world.

Here are two lessons I learned the hard way. A few days after you retire from business, you are almost forgotten, and, unless you're Tiger Woods, nobody (not even your spouse) cares about your golf scores. But another lesson I learned is this: Use your business skills to help others and share the gospel, and you will always be important in the lives of others.

As the following chapters show, there are incredible benefits to be had when the church joins the business community to support SCAs, MFIs, and other employment-based solutions that are already having a significant impact on reducing physical and spiritual poverty.

15

WAYS TO WORK
FOR GOD

(PHIL)

An innovative project was conceived by Tulsa Bible Church in conjunction with the Slavic Gospel Association and the Volgodonsk Baptist Church. They decided to have a "seminary" in Volgodonsk, Russia, by having teachers fly from Tulsa to Russia on a regular basis and teach for two weeks. The seminary teachers were either trained professionals or ordinary church members who became specialists in one topic. More than forty Russians received the equivalent of seminary training in this way. There was one major hitch — the same hitch that has plagued the church's international efforts for the last hundred years. How will these indigenous preachers survive financially without foreign churches paying their support well into the future? Unfortunately, this is a widespread conundrum played out in many ministries.

The problem is summarized by one author: "In the last 50 years the church ... appears to be almost exclusively focused on a model that assumes the need for donations to finance ministry. The church in North America has taught this model to the rest of the world, and the formula of depending on donations is accepted everywhere. But the perception that ministry requires offerings creates great limitations for ministry. This is especially true in countries where donations are scarce."[1]

One of the biggest hindrances to evangelistic efforts in developing countries is the lack of money to pay for sustained projects. An associated problem is that it is extremely difficult for organizations and individuals initially supported by outside donations to wean themselves off the aid. One way to overcome both of these problems is to have missionaries and other Christian workers improve their incomes in a sustainable manner.

Improving the incomes of missionaries and churches can be a double-edged sword. On one edge, the improved incomes increase their sense of freedom and the options available to them for making and training disciples. Their "tent-making" activities (Acts 18:2 – 3) may even pave the way for long-term acceptance in the local business community. Yet the time and energy needed to improve income may take time and energy away from other vital efforts. Furthermore, as in America, some preachers who excel at sharing the gospel have defective genes in entrepreneurship.

You might have noticed that I use the term "improve" income instead of "increase" income. In developing countries, increasing income is only one aspect of improving income. As an example, income can be increased by growing sales while reducing costs. In a different way, incomes can be improved if they become more reliable and more frequent. For people living hand to mouth, having an income of $2 every day is better than having $10 every fifth day. Long-term incomes might also be improved if someone attains a better competitive situation or gets more business training. Incomes also improve when someone's personal dignity and security is increased by having a job instead of depending on outsiders for charity, even if the total amount of money remains the same. In the developing world, income is much more than a number on a monthly income statement.

We need to be clear: while the following techniques are applicable for indigenous missionaries, they may be less suitable for those sent from America. Many missionaries sent from America will continue to be supported by donations and salaries from America. This is all the more reason why the church should strive harder to have more indigenous missionaries.

CHURCH-OWNED BUSINESSES

Churches have long operated businesses such as bookstores, medical clinics, and schools. Sometimes churches do not charge for these services, sometimes they charge small fees, and other times they charge enough to make the businesses self-sustaining or even profitable.

One of my favorite businesses of this type is in Florence, Italy. There you can find the perfumery of the church of Santa Maria Novella. It is a specialty store providing perfumes and handmade soaps and lotions. It is as upscale as anything you would see on the best streets in Paris or New York. It originally started as the herb garden for the monks of the nearby cathedral. The business has been so successful it has far outgrown its original location and purpose.

If a church decides to have significant income from a service, it should consider moving the administration of the service into a different organization with separate management, oversight, and accounting. This will allow all parties to clearly differentiate responsibilities and goals and may even allow the service provider an opportunity to gather new donations or support from other organizations.

Although separating the service from the church might be a needed step, history has shown that this often results in the daughter organization becoming totally independent and modifying its purpose and mission until it no longer correlates to those of the founding church — not unlike what occasionally happens with our own daughters.

BUSINESS TRAINING

Business training teaches the skills needed for bookkeeping, accounting, marketing, and management — skills needed by any small business owner. American businesspeople can help transfer these skills to indigenous entrepreneurs, but these skills may need to be radically altered to be applicable in the informal economies of developing countries. A good rule of thumb is that the higher the income of the people in question, the more complex the business training can be. On one end of the spectrum are people who are illiterate and live on less than $1 per day. On the other end are businesspeople living in communities in developing countries which may be more advanced than some American cities.

In many countries, illiteracy keeps people from understanding the basics of business. For instance, in Haiti only about half of the population over the age of fifteen can read and write. In rural areas, the problem is far greater. Many nonprofit organizations and microfinance institutions must attack this problem before offering their services.

The microfinance institution Esperanza found illiteracy to be a problem when they began operating in Haiti. In a small, dimly lit room in Trou du Nord, a borrower group met to receive their first loans. The loan officer became aware of the problem as the new borrowers pretended to read the contracts and then sign their names. They were obviously unfamiliar with a ballpoint pen, and most were unable to sign their own names and used the ubiquitous "X." How could these borrowers be expected to grow their businesses without basic literacy skills?

In countries where illiteracy is less of a problem, MFIs often need to teach the basics of capitalism and how to obtain capital. Dave McCabe distributes gaskets, motor packings, and mechanical seals in America. On a trip to Russia, he found that many people in the local church had small businesses but had no concept of marketing. He returned home and designed a marketing program which was viable for use in their community. When he got the chance to teach the course in a university, he found a very interested audience. However, after the class was over, he asked how people intended to use the material. Without exception, the students had found

the theory interesting but never expected to have enough capital to start their own businesses. Such situations illustrate the need for relationships with Westerners having business expertise and investment capital.

JOB TRAINING

Done appropriately, job training is an excellent way to help people improve their incomes. Many Americans have the ability to help improve job skills or production techniques of others. With only a little more training, information, or tools, it is possible for someone to become more productive in their work. Providing these things is often inexpensive. As I finished writing this paragraph, my wife returned from a silversmith class. The few things she learned in four hours will make her much more productive and creative. Imagine how a master jeweler or expert welder or master mechanic could do the same for workers around the world.

The first step in providing job training is determining what jobs are available or can be made profitable. For instance, if enough people in an area must take their welding needs to a distant town, there might be sufficient need for a welder in the community. There is no need for ten welders. I recently met with an American church that had hired a Honduran preacher who had promised he had enough job skills to provide for much of his income. Imagine everyone's dismay when they found out that he was an automobile mechanic and they had moved him to a Honduran community with very few cars.

I was once on a missions committee that sent support for many years to an effort in India. The American couple running the program had special skills as a machinist and a nurse. They were unable to enter the country as missionaries, but they were able to enter and stay in the country for many years because of the school they built that not only trained badly needed machinists but also made a special effort to recruit and train physically handicapped people.

Americans in developing countries have to be careful of unintended consequences when we get involved in job training. I once heard an expert say, "Job-training programs have done immense damage to the poor in developing countries." I was incredulous until he explained his logic (which applies to America as well). He explained that job training is such an obvious way to help people that many donors and governments spend huge amounts of money on job training. These job-training programs are often set up to encourage people to attend by paying a daily stipend. From an American's viewpoint, this is an appropriate and expected course of action. Yet many people in developing countries go from program to program just to collect these stipends. In addition, these programs often train people for jobs that *don't even exist* in their communities.

This demand-and-supply issue often happens at the borrower level in microfinance. For instance, a woman might be a very skilled seamstress who has to spend an inordinate amount of time doing mundane seams or stitches. It might make sense for her to use a microloan to buy a sewing machine and then receive training in its use. Before doing so, however, it is a good idea to determine if there is enough of a market for her increased amount of production. If not, and another market can't be found, she may find that she will have to take on an additional job with her new-found time just to pay for the sewing machine.

ANIMAL "LOANS"

Heifer International has a proven method of helping farmers around the world. After many years, the organization has learned it must analyze the needs and opportunities of a community before embarking on any project of size since tiny markets are easily oversaturated. After finding the right situation, it selects farmers and trains them in the appropriate ways to raise and care for a particular type of animal. That training may include improving pastureland or building sheds or cages. Heifer International then "loans" the cows, sheep, chickens, or another type of animal to the people it has trained. Rather than walking away and assuming its work is finished, the farmers' progress is monitored and adjustments are made as needed. Finally, the farmers "repay" the loans by passing on one or more of the animals' offspring to other needy farmers in the community.

Bud Pederson is a missionary in Asia. He came to realize the risks of depending on American donors to provide "lifetime support" for the indigenous missionaries in his area. Bud's solution was to raise enough money to purchase a few water buffalo. Through their milk, meat, and calves, these animals now provide a large percentage of the livelihoods of the indigenous preachers he works with.

BUSINESS INCUBATION

In the course of an American church's relationship with a foreign church, certain large business opportunities might become apparent. This might simply involve providing capital, or it might require some access to a new market or new equipment or manufacturing techniques. If someone is willing to take ownership of the project, it might make sense for outsiders to provide the missing pieces and help local people start new businesses. In some cases it might make sense for the outsiders to own the business until it becomes profitable, and then sell it to the locals.

During their missions trip to Russia, Sergei convinced some American Christians that he could build a trucking business if they would loan him the money to buy a truck. His business plan seemed sound, so they loaned him many thousands of dollars. His plan worked well and he paid back their loan according to their agreement. Sergei had the experience and talent to make the business work well. Sergei knew the local business climate in intimate detail—something which is nearly impossible to do from America.

Some other business incubation ideas don't work out so well. Jeff Rutt's story has always intrigued me because he learned some important lessons from a failed business incubation project. This experience eventually provided the happy ending of the story of the Calvary Monument Bible Church in Lancaster, Pennsylvania, in chapter 3.

Jeff and his associates conducted several feasibility studies to determine some self-sustaining ways for a church in Ukraine to reduce its dependency on Jeff's home church in Pennsylvania. After formulating more than fifty business models, they settled on one involving the processing of oil from sunflower seeds. The church purchased a machine for $2,000 and shipped it to Ukraine.

Jeff and his colleagues had thought of all the possible problems and had all the bases covered. He absolutely knew the plan would work. Except it didn't. A year later, Jeff returned to Ukraine and found that the machine had never been used. After confronting the church leaders, Jeff contritely learned that a foolproof plan in Lancaster, Pennsylvania, may be proof of the plan of a fool in Ukraine. Jeff's team made two simple but fatal errors. First, the business plan was written in English, and nobody took the time to translate it. Second, and more important, the church leaders had no interest in making and selling sunflower seed oil. They did not believe there was a market for the product and didn't want to waste their time. Whether there really *was* a market was unimportant. Without the support of the church leaders, the project was doomed to fail. Jeff and his friends started over and decided to use microfinance to help their Ukrainian friends create their own business models — and the result was HOPE International.

CAUTION

One final word of caution: Jesus often spoke about the impossibility of loving both God and money. "No one can serve two masters. Either you will hate the one and love the other, or you will be devoted to the one and despise the other. You cannot serve both God and Money" (Luke 16:13 TNIV). Given his warnings, we would be wise to recognize the slow, seductive pull of money and success. Missionaries and business leaders would be wise to be attentive to the dangers inherent in business and ensure that the work of ministry continues.

Unfortunately, history shows that many ministries started with the best of intentions are no longer concerned with Christian witness. It is necessary to always keep in mind that helping people improve their incomes should be integrated with ways of improving their spiritual lives.

It is becoming imperative that the church in America find ways to share the gospel in developing countries while simultaneously finding creative ways to help new Christians and churches become self-supporting. This is difficult because so many evangelistic efforts involve people living in extreme poverty. However, if the church does not accomplish this, many of its efforts will be for naught in the long term as local churches wither and fade. In an effort to keep this from occurring, some Christians are taking individual responsibility by using their own businesses.

16

GOING CORPORATE
FOR THE POOR

(PHIL)

"Unashamedly Ethical" is the motto of a South African construction and development company named The Power Group. Founded by Graham Power in 1983, the company recently celebrated twenty-five years of uninterrupted business success. However, according to the company's literature, they are only a quarter of the way through their 100-year goal of improving lives throughout Africa.

The Power Group has an impressive record of excellent construction and property development projects, but more impressive to me are their accomplishments going beyond mere financial or infrastructure successes: the companies of the Power Group donate the first 10 percent of their profits to the Power Group Charitable Fund. The fund supports various charitable organizations as designated by their board of trustees and was inspired by Proverbs 3:9 – 10, which instructs followers of God to "Honor the Lord with your wealth, with the firstfruits of all your crops; then your barns will be filled to overflowing, and your vats will brim over with new wine" (TNIV). Its HIV program tests all employees, provides instruction on preventing the disease, and encourages treatment for those who are infected. It also sponsors the Beautiful Gate Ministry, which is an international interdenominational Christian organization providing medical, emotional, spiritual, and physical care to children suffering from HIV and AIDs. Its Eagles Rising Training Centre is involved in training youth from the poorest informal settlements in Cape Town. It offers Christian discipleship and skills training on both a part-time and full-time basis. One of my friends who attended a meeting at the center was overwhelmed with the focus on prayer and worship.

Graham Power also founded Transformation Africa and the associated Global Day of Prayer. In June 1999, he received a vision that he resisted because of his lack of formal theological training. After all, he reasoned, "I am just a businessman." However, in 2001 he rented the Newlands Rugby Stadium where 45,000 Christians from all denominations and races came together to pray for Cape Town's rising crime rate, poor rainfall, and bomb attacks. The prayer movement quickly expanded across Africa and the world. In 2007, millions of Christians from 204 nations united in the Global Day of Prayer.

Graham Power and The Power Group are one example of a growing international movement known as Business as Missions (BAM) that is changing the developing world.

Business as Missions was described in detail at the Lausanne Committee for World Evangelization held in Thailand in 2004. The Lausanne Movement is an international movement committed to energizing "the whole Church to take the whole gospel to the whole world." It was born out of the First International Congress on World Evangelization called by Billy Graham and held in Switzerland in July 1974. The structure of the organization allows it to examine more than thirty issues which are of significant concern in taking the good news to the world. An issue group committee specifically studied the topic of Business as Missions and wrote that the basic premise underlying this concept is that "God calls people to work for His kingdom in business just as certainly as He calls people to work in other kinds of ministry or mission ventures."[1]

Business as Missions is a very broad term, but as it concerns developing countries, BAM generally means a for-profit business which is formed specifically to demonstrate Christian principles and practices to employees, customers, and suppliers and to improve the income and infrastructure of the surrounding community — all to the greater glory of God. Other names which might be used for this concept include transformational business, Great Commission business, and kingdom business.

BAM ventures are typically founded by people who have or can obtain both the money and talent to start and run a business as well as a vision for using those gifts to improve lives in the developing world. The business might be located in a developing country, or it might be located in America in order to do business with developing countries around the world. The basic difference between a BAM and any other business is the intentional desire to demonstrate Christian principles. This does not mean that a BAM must run evangelistic projects, but that the business intends to exemplify the gospel of Christ. BAM ventures have the potential to improve the image and reception of Christianity in hostile communities around the world as they bring the universally accepted benefits of employment and profit to the local market.

Many American businesspeople have long felt alienated from the Christian community. Business as Missions provides these people a direct way to integrate practical Christianity with their current skills and talents. More and more Americans have developed skills and relationships that allow them to work effectively in developing countries. Consider the following advantages of a Business as Missions venture that might attract skilled businesspeople:

- Many BAMs focus on larger businesses which generate many jobs. Christians living in developing countries may have an extra incentive for being employed by one of these businesses since they might be discriminated against by those in other companies who practice other religions.

- BAMs have the potential to alleviate poverty in other ways than providing jobs. By bringing outside capital and expertise into a community, a BAM can improve the job skills of its employees, improve the incomes of other businesses, and help provide information about markets and international needs to other agencies and organizations.

- Businesses may seem to have more long-term commitment to an area than missionaries or other evangelical activities, a perception that provides businesspeople an easier opportunity to develop long-term relationships within the community.

- Some countries are averse to allowing missionaries or overt evangelical activities, but they usually welcome businesses that will increase the tax base and provide true economic development.

- If a BAM is done well, it demonstrates an integrated Christian lifestyle to a watching community. These businesses provide the context to share the gospel in word and deed to employees, suppliers, and customers.

- "If there is no indigenous church, business as mission can be a powerful part of the strategic plan for church planting ... Kingdom businesses provide the local church and new disciples with models that they can easily understand and replicate. A new believer can relate to and learn from someone who is working out their Christianity in daily work life just like them. To the local church, the principle of empowerment, sustainability and multiplication is modeled rather than dependency. In turn, new Christian businesspeople are affirmed, strengthened and released to serve God and His kingdom through business."[2]

Calvin Burgess is the CEO of Dominion Farms Ltd., based in Guthrie,

Oklahoma. Dominion has a farm in Kenya that is its first venture in Africa. According to an open letter, the project encompasses over 17,000 acres on the equator near Lake Victoria. The property was a low-lying area, subject to frequent flooding and in need of a tremendous amount of work and capital. It was a failed government project that lay dormant for many years. Since acquiring the property, Dominion Farms has constructed a significant dam with hydroelectric capability, many miles of dykes, a water storage reservoir of 1,100 acres, a housing compound, grain storage and drying facilities, workshops, and many miles of roads. They expect the project to eventually produce up to 100,000 metric tons of rice annually, which is almost half of the amount of rice that Kenya imports each year. Dominion has constructed classrooms, medical clinics, public roads, water wells, markets, and sports fields for the local community. It also provides a moral and spiritual example to the community. Calvin states, "The mis-

sionaries, medical teams, and government aid have all gone to Africa. It is now time for the business community to come and make its presence felt." I will return to the story of Dominion Farms later in the chapter.

Ben Roberts uses BAM to change the world on a smaller but equally important scale. Ben attends a church that oversees projects in Vietnam, which is a restricted Communist country. Through his several trips to Vietnam, Ben has met many young artists who are immensely talented but have no forum for their work. They currently make a meager living by creating reproduction art for tourists. Ben and his colleagues partner with these artists by offering their original works over the Internet and other outlets to the American market. They are able to offer original works and limited prints for the same price as mass-produced art. Ten percent of the profits are committed to the mission of serving Vietnam. One of their unique ideas is to burn art that hasn't sold in one year, which was the genesis for the name of their website, *www.GlobalArtInferno.org*.

ARE BAMs EFFECTIVE?

Mark L. Russell writes, "Globalization is radically changing social structures and government policies. Missions must adapt to these new realities. BAM is one of the more exciting and innovative developments in missions, using a new approach that recognizes both the centrality of employment to people's lives as well as the reality of a new world.[3]

Russell surveyed twelve BAMs in Thailand, a primarily Buddhist country. He found that the companies had two types of primary tendencies regarding the sharing of the good news. The first type had a low-key holistic approach and concentrated on providing an environment in which to expose their employees to the lifestyle of a Jesus follower. They also brought in supporting organizations, including local pastors, to help in the other parts of the disciple-making process. These companies were both successful in making Christ disciples and in keeping employees satisfied.

The second type of company tried to overtly use their business primarily as an evangelistic tool to achieve conversions to Christianity. These companies struggled to be effective in either sharing the gospel message or in having satisfied employees. Russell concluded that the first type of company was forty-eight times more likely to make disciples than the second type.

Some of Russell's findings also support the thought that business is capable of creating a uniquely conducive environment to tell people about Jesus. After interviewing twenty-six converts, he found that each one had two common factors: they had been exposed to Christian demonstration over an extended period of time, and they had been exposed consistently during that time. Here's the kicker: the typical time frame needed was exposure for five days a week for about five years. If these people had been exposed only on Sundays, the time of conversion would have been much, much longer.

While Business as Missions ventures are exploding in popularity, Christians need to ask several hard questions. Due to some inherent qualities of business ventures, they may actually be riskier than proponents like to admit. Anyone interested in beginning or supporting a BAM should consider the following cautions and concerns:

- BAM is best suited for one role in the disciple-making process — demonstrating a Christian lifestyle. Therefore, the disciple-making process will be best completed if it acts in a coordinated manner with other organizations, especially local churches.

- By its very nature, every BAM is a unique organization which is dependent on specific owners and managers. It is difficult to replicate a particular organization in other locations or countries.

- A BAM might cause unintended damage. For instance, in most developing countries, the production and distribution of food is inefficient and provides employment for many people. If you started a supermarket in many cities, you could probably reduce the inefficiencies in the system and make a profit. In doing so, you might also provide a wider selection of cheaper food to your customers and provide fifty new jobs, all of which would be wonderful for poverty alleviation. However, you might also unwittingly reduce the income and destroy the jobs of hundreds of people in the local economy and partially destabilize the community.

- The managers and owners of these companies have two objectives which may come into conflict. The first objective is to make a profit. To make a profit, owners and managers will find it difficult to consistently demonstrate Christian principles and practices to all parties, both inside and outside the company. These difficulties will arise no matter how pure the intention to act properly because there are a nearly infinite number of ways to demonstrate Christian principles and practices. For instance, once a profit is made, how should profits be shared among the owners and employees? Should prices be reduced so customers benefit? Should all the profits be donated to local churches? What appears to be Christian witness to one person may appear to be hypocrisy to another.

- Because the intention to overtly share the gospel and the teachings of the Bible vary greatly among BAMs, it is not always clear how local churches can work in conjunction with them.

- These businesses are privately owned and many fail. Success in business is determined by depth of capital commitment, management abilities, market acceptance, and many other factors. In America, the majority of new businesses fail within four years. There is no reason to think the market will be any kinder in developing countries. Acknowledging God in your business's charter statement is no guarantee of success. Just because the owner has good intentions does not mean either the market or God will make sure the business succeeds. Normal business laws control these businesses as well as all others. A failed BAM has the potential to do immense damage to the image of Christ, the local church, and other Christians.

Now that I have described some possible problems with BAM, let's return to the story earlier in this chapter about Dominion Farms' large project in Kenya. I have every reason to believe that the project is valid and the owners have invested millions of dollars primarily to help the people of Kenya. However, only time will tell if that is true. In the mean time, we should be sensitive to how others might criticize such a project and, as a result, bring suspicion to the cause of Christ. For instance, does the purchase of 17,000 acres represent in any way the confiscation of property from those who have been customarily using it, even if they didn't own

legal title? Wouldn't some native people and organizations prefer the continued existence of a swamp rather than having a farm? Even if Dominion Farms reinvests its profits in the project, might they still be criticized for paying too little for the labor of its employees? With these types of questions you can see that virtually any project has the potential to backfire or be criticized.

In the end, the effectiveness of any BAM will depend on the execution of the intentions of the owners of the company. To learn more about Business as Missions, your time will be well-spent reading *God Is at Work* by Ken Eldred, and *Business as Mission, Occasional Paper No. 59* by the Lausanne Committee for World Evangelization. In addition, there are organizations which encourage and train Christian businesspeople to become involved in BAM and other forms of business assistance. Two of these are Integra (*www.integrausa.org*) and Partners Worldwide (*www.partnersworldwide.org*).

17

ROLLING UP OUR SLEEVES

(PHIL)

How many times did you think about poverty last week? The prophet Amos had harsh words for Israel, calling them "cows of Bashan" (Amos 4:1) for neglecting the poor. Amos outlines God's distaste for the way they "oppress the poor and crush the needy" (v. 1) and warns, "Though you have built stone mansions, you will not live in them; though you have planted lush vineyards, you will not drink their wine" (Amos 5:11). Forgetting the poor is unthinkable to God.

Yet for us, forgetting is all too easy. We do not see the poor men in Zambia when we leave our suburban homes and drive to work. We do not see the poor children in Cambodia during our lunch breaks. We might see the poor women in Peru only on television — but it's easy to change the channel.

This is why we need reminders. This is why the pages of our Bibles — from Genesis to the prophets of the Israelites, and from Jesus to Paul — consistently command us to remember the poor. Turning a blind eye is sinful, but it is quick and painless, particularly since we live in a culture where we're bombarded by three thousand commercials every day showing us what *we* don't have.[1] They shout the lie that we'd be more popular, sexy, and satisfied if only we had a better outfit, cell phone, flat screen, or

car. What we really need are constant reminders of what we *do* have and how we can act to impact those who have far less. Maybe then we will roll up our sleeves and actually do something about it.

LESS IS MORE

Tony Campolo is considered by some to be a modern-day William Wilberforce with regard to social justice issues. He is a living reminder not to forget the poor. Unconventional in his approach, Campolo is focused on pricking the evangelical conscience in order to prompt action for the poor. In *Everybody Wants to Change the World*, Campolo and Gordon Aeschliman describe one movement designed to help us remember the poor.

One simple idea for combating compassion fatigue is to try to live once a month on less than one dollar a day, like nearly two million people do every day. Commit to doing this for a year with a group of friends who also want to go on the same spiritual journey of keeping the poor alive in their hearts. After the year is up, evaluate how the discipline has shaped your lifestyle and commitments regarding the needs of the poor. Living on less than one dollar will be a challenge because you will have to deprive your body for twenty-four hours. You will have to fast for the day — or eat a can of soup that you purchased for less than one dollar. Your beverage will consist of glasses of water from the faucet. And you won't be able to drive far, because you'd use up a dollar's worth of fuel in a short distance.

Another modern-day reminder is Mike Foster and his creative team that serve at Ethur, a nonprofit arm of PlainJoe Studios. They created the Junky Car Club in the spring of 2006 to help people move beyond consumerism and toward increased generosity. The club was founded when Foster sold his fully loaded Infiniti G35 sports car to drive a "junky" 1993 Toyota Camry and invited his friends to do the same. Members of the Junky Car Club agree to drive cheap cars so they can better steward their resources to help the poor. Junky Car Club members describe themselves as "a bunch of happy drivers who are politely rebelling against consumerism by driving junky cars." Club members are encouraged to use their money in service to the disadvantaged instead of making excessive car payments. Since its inception, the Junky Car Club has registered members in the United States, Australia, Russia, England, New Zealand, Scotland, and Singapore.[2]

Christmas may be the best time of the year to engage children in remembering the example and life of Jesus instead of celebrating consumerism gone crazy. Followers of Jesus could use this time of the year to focus on the joys that come from giving to others and restore a degree of sanity to the holiday. Jen Knepper of Pennsylvania celebrates Christmas with all seven of her nieces and nephews by pulling together a portion of their allowances that they have saved throughout the year and looking through the materials of Heifer International, World Vision, and Samaritan's Purse to pick out gifts to give to others around the world. During the Christmas season, the Alternative Gift Fair (*www.theladieshalf.org/giftsthatgive.html*) is attempting to give people giving opportunities with service-focused organizations. Instead of shopping mania on Black Friday, the Alternative Gift Fair orchestrates fairs where shoppers can purchase gift cards supporting local and international charities. All of these types of efforts are attempting to combat the perception of many Americans who "honestly think we have barely enough to survive in modest comfort."[3]

VOLUNTEERING

Another way to remember the poor in developing countries is through volunteering. PEER Servants is an organization connecting volunteers directly to microfinance institutions around the world. By breaking individuals into teams that maximize the skills and abilities of each member, they have proven meaningful engagement is possible, even from a distance.

Take the example of Kay Walsh who serves as the communications di-

rector for PEER Servants. As an administrative assistant in the Center for Environmental Health Services at the Massachusetts Institute of Technology (MIT), there is no question she has technical, creative, and managerial gifts. In her spare time — ha! — Kay oversees the PEER Servants website, promotional materials, and event presentations. This volunteer position with PEER Servants allows her to use her many skills for making Christ's love for the poor known. She explains it this way: "It took a long time for me to find a ministry where I could apply so many of my talents and experience to help further the Kingdom. Our work and our ministry meetings are fun, holy, and fruitful, and praise God that I'm part of a community of Christian businesspeople, since I've been a business owner and can understand the struggles of an entrepreneur."[4]

PEER Servants is a leader in connecting volunteers to ministry opportunities, but many other organizations provide opportunities as well, and several do so through relationships with the Halftime movement. As previously described, Bob Buford's book *Halftime* inspired thousands of individuals in the second half of their lives to seek service opportunities. Many of these individuals have business skills critical to building employment-based solutions to poverty. Since microfinance is essentially banking for the poor, it is a natural place for bankers and the business community to devote their skills to a very different group of shareholders. The same skills that led to success in the first half of life can be applied in amazing ways in the second half.

Dale Dawson is one such individual who serves as a dedicated volunteer and board member with Opportunity International. During the first half of his life, Dale's work ethic and business acumen led to his success as head of Investment Banking at Stephens Inc., an investment firm in Arkansas, and as the major stockholder and CEO of TruckPro, the nation's largest distributor of truck and trailer parts. Now in the second half of his career, Dale uses the skills and experience he gained as a businessman to improve and expand microfinance services in Rwanda and other African countries.

ON YOUR KNEES, PLEASE

How often do we say "I'll pray for you" — and how often do we really pray? In Scripture, prayer is often like a wrestling match. As pastor and author Rick Warren writes,

> People may refuse our love or reject our message, but they are defenseless against our prayers. The Bible tells us to pray for opportunities to witness, for courage to speak up, for those who will believe, for the rapid spread of the message, and for more … Get a globe or map and pray for nations by name. Also, pray for missionaries and everyone else involved in the global harvest. Paul told his prayer partners, "You are also joining to help us when you pray for us."[5]

Prayer focuses us on what is important. Praying for those in poverty can open our eyes to their reality and connect our hearts with theirs. In an amazing way, prayer has the potential to change us even as we are praying for others. James writes, "The prayer of a righteous person is powerful and effective" (James 5:16 TNIV). Our prayers are heard by a loving God who loves to respond. Consider joining the prayer update list of missions-minded microfinance organizations and remembering staff, employees, and clients in regular prayer.

LEARN TOGETHER

Your small group or church can easily learn more about the biblical understanding of poverty, its causes, and its remedies. Some of what you and your fellow Christians find may spur you into action. Here are a few helpful resources:

- *Hope Lives* is a curriculum written by Compassion International staff member Amber Van Schooneveld. There is an accompanying Pastor's Guide, Sermon Clips on DVD, and Tools for the Pastor on CD-ROM.

This kit equips pastors, like Todd Nathan at Calvary Church, to facilitate a five-week series with small groups.[6] Nathan describes how this curriculum had a transformational impact as his small group explored the issues of poverty for the first time.

- Produced jointly between the Episcopal Church and the Evangelical Lutheran Church in America, the study *God's Mission in the World: An Ecumenical Christian Study Guide on Global Poverty and the Millennium Development Goals* offers a unique approach to poverty from an ecumenical perspective. This guide was released as part of the ONE Episcopalian Campaign and features six weekly sessions examining Christian understanding of social justice, global poverty, and the Millennium Development Goals (MDGs).[7] These goals were developed by United Nations member states and leading international organizations and include cutting extreme poverty in half, reducing child mortality rates, fighting disease epidemics such as AIDS, and developing a global partnership for development by 2015.[8]

- Given the relative paucity of biblically based curricula that explore Scripture's teaching on the poor and our response, Peter Greer, his father, and Willowdale Chapel created a set of materials designed for small groups. It focuses in greater detail on the problem of poverty and how Scripture calls people of God to respond. It is available at *www.thepoorwillbeglad.com.*

SEE IT TO BELIEVE IT

Sometimes you need to see something to understand it. Greg Thompson, an entrepreneur from Massachusetts, described the impact of seeing microfinance firsthand: "I had heard about microfinance, but was blown away when I actually saw it. It was like watching fireworks on television versus actually being underneath the explosions … like watching a movie about a roller coaster versus being in the front seat of one. It's just so much more incredible in person."[9]

These experiences can prompt individuals to take significant action. Justin Bredeman was an executive with Auntie Anne's pretzel-franchising company prior to traveling to the Dominican Republic to learn about microfinance along with me and several others. He explained, "Meeting individuals who were working themselves out of poverty, hearing their stories firsthand, visiting their homes and meeting their children had a much bigger impact on me than I ever expected. There is a way of helping people help themselves, and I wanted to be a part of it." Shortly after this first trip, Justin left his corporate career and joined HOPE International full time.

But what should you do when you return from a short-term mission trip to an impoverished community? Is it enough to return from a trip and feel more thankful for all that you have? That's a start. But if that is the only fruit after direct encounter with poverty, something is missing. Seeing such needs with our own eyes creates a responsibility to actually *do* something.

Unfortunately, the statistics are not encouraging about the way short-term trips move people to action. Kurt Ver Beek, director of Calvin College's Honduras Program, has dedicated a significant part of his research to the effectiveness of short-term missions. In a recent interview, *Christianity Today* magazine reported on his findings:

> While 52 percent of respondents claimed to have increased their giving to the sending organization after the trip, according to the organization's records 70 percent of the participants in their STM [short-term mission] trips to Honduras didn't send in a single direct donation in the three years after the trip ... [and] few lasting friendships were built. While 92 percent of the North Americans said they had meaningful contact with Hondurans for at least part of every day of their trip, less than a quarter stayed in touch with their Honduran friends after they returned home.[10]

Although the results found by Ver Beek may not reflect the impact of every short-term mission trip, there is no doubt that short-term missions are exploding in popularity. There ought to be a way to find ways to discover which people were truly impacted by their experience and engage them quickly after the trip. We are missing a big opportunity if the church does not find better ways to translate these positive experiences into long-term action.

GIVING WITH EXCELLENCE

The primary way most of us engage the poor in developing countries is through giving. Two thousand years ago, the apostle Paul told the church members at Corinth that they already excelled "in everything — in faith, in speech, in knowledge, in complete earnestness and in your love for us" (2 Corinthians 8:7). Then he went on to exhort them to "see that you also excel in this grace of giving" (v. 7). How can we twenty-first-century Christians excel at the grace of giving?

Don Millican is the CFO of a successful company, a former partner of a "Big Four" accounting firm, and a long-time church leader. He asks some clarifying questions about excellent giving. Does it mean to give effectively? If so, how do we define effectiveness and gather the data to measure it? Does it mean to give according to what we feel are the leadings of the Holy Spirit? If so, how do we quantify those leadings and implement them in our lives? How do we even understand how we fit in the process of giving?

Millican points to 1 Corinthians 3:6 – 7 as an important passage showing that God is responsible for the results of our giving, not us. "I planted the seed, Apollos watered it, but God made it grow. So neither he who plants nor he who waters is anything, but only God, who makes things grow." From our earthly point of view we cannot see how effective some programs have been, are, or may be in the future. Millican asks, "What if you only impact one person for Christ, and that person turns out to be the next Billy Graham?"

He also says we are to be good stewards of the resources entrusted to us, and, in that capacity, we have to make the best giving decisions we can, given the information we have. Being an excellent giver often means living at the intersection of faith and action.

Our giving resources consist of time, talent, and treasure. If we think about it this way, we realize that our time and talent are mostly constrained by our physical location. For that reason, our time and talent are often best allocated mostly to our local communities. Our treasure is our "stored labor." We can easily ship our stored labor anywhere in the world at any time. So, if efficiency is the point, our treasure is often the resource best used in developing countries.

Our treasure doesn't consist only of the money residing in our bank accounts. We Americans have many unexpected sources of treasure available if we just look around for them. The high school leadership group at First United Methodist Church in Birmingham, Michigan, met one afternoon in 2005. They decided to implement a new project to reach their own community about the problem of HIV and AIDS in Africa. Their plan was to collect 23 million pennies representing the 23 million people infected with HIV and AIDS in sub-Saharan Africa. These funds will sponsor several African health and educational organizations. With this Penny Project, FUMC youth are changing the world one penny at a time. At the beginning of 2009, they had collected 21 million pennies![11]

After a lot of head-banging and Scripture study, Don Millican and I have come to understand that the Bible seems to address three categories of giving. As we allocate resources between and within these categories, we must rely on the Holy Spirit to lead us and guide us through prayer, the wise counsel of church leaders and other Christians, and the still, small voice that we occasionally hear.

- *Church.* A portion of our giving should go to the local group of Christians with whom we meet regularly. These monies are placed with the congregation's leaders who have been chosen by God. As members of the community, we are called to rely on the group's leadership and support its prayerful actions. This type of giving makes up the majority of giving for many American Christians, and it also made up the majority of giving for Jews and Christians in the early days of the church. The responsibility for how effectively these gifts are spent primarily belongs to the leadership, not to the givers.

- *Compassion.* We are called to compassionately meet the immediate needs of people in our lives, especially our families and other Christians. Although we are supposed to meet needs, we must be

careful not to create dependency. In this type of giving, we are to rely on the Holy Spirit to help us be discerning in how we meet these needs. Our end goal is to see that needs are met and that God receives the glory.

- *Calling.* We are individually called to spread the kingdom by helping people, both physically and spiritually. Those of us who are rich — and that's *all* of us! — have the ability to make a significant and lasting impact in impoverished countries.

But how specifically should we allocate our resources to make a difference for Jesus Christ? How do we put biblical principles and commandments into action? The allocation of our resources is where we roll up our sleeves and put our money where our mouths are.

I'd like to offer some ideas based on the histories of my giving and those of people and churches I have worked with over the last several years. The most common characteristic of givers (and missions committees) is to give money away this year very much like it was given the previous year. Sometimes this happens after intensive analysis, but more often it happens for a variety of other reasons such as habit, the desire not to hurt somebody's feelings, or to be responsive to pleas from friends.

Our actions would be entirely different if we chose to follow clear guidelines. For instance, in the past I have chosen to allocate money based on the effectiveness of individual projects, but now I try to allocate based on a project's ability to help people both spiritually and physically on a long-term basis. Because I have changed my guidelines, the results of how I give have changed dramatically.

As an example, consider an evangelist who might propose going to India and presenting the gospel to ten thousand people over two weeks at a cost of $20,000. He believes he will be able to preach to that number of people but has not coordinated the effort with local Christians for follow-up relationship building. In the past I would have found this to be a good project because sharing the gospel at $2 per person seems very efficient. Today I would not support the project because by definition it would not meet people's physical and spiritual needs over the long term.

Let me point out that I (or a missions committee or a benevolence committee) will spend a giving budget using some method and some set of assumptions. The fact that the money gets spent means that value judgments and allocations techniques are being made and used, whether explicitly or implicitly. Since every giving expenditure is evaluated in *some* way, doesn't it make sense to evaluate our choices thoughtfully and intentionally? Some people believe their allocations and judgments are made solely through the leading of the Holy Spirit, but taking the time to apply prayerful wisdom and thought to our giving decisions is simply a way of fulfilling the steward responsibility God has given us.

Here's some good news that we hope this book has made clear. Microfinance and a few other employment-based poverty alleviation solutions are often the most cost-effective way to help those living in poverty. Giving to these types of projects and to the right organizations is the least risky and most beneficial way to improve the physical and spiritual condition of impoverished people around the world. We don't need to be afraid of giving. Rather, as we see the holistic work being done by brave Christians in every country around the world, our only fear may be that we aren't yet giving enough.

CHOOSING ORGANIZATIONS

I believe givers should ask themselves two basic questions when they start assessing whether to support an organization. First, are my goals and the goals of the organization in harmony? Second, does the organization actually try to achieve its stated goals in a way that makes sense to me?

The first question became apparent to me after giving a speech about microfinance. When it was over, a woman chided me with, "All you care about is poor people. I care most about eliminating abuse to pets." Obviously, she and I should support different organizations.

The second question became important to me after I started asking people why the organizations they worked with or supported, some of which were churches, should be considered "Christian." Here are the types of answers I typically received: "Because we feed the poor and Jesus said we should do that"; "Because we provide fresh water for people which makes their lives better"; "Because some of our field personnel share the gospel when they think the time is right"; "Because the founders of our organizations were Baptists"; and, "Because some of our board members go to church regularly." These types of answers remind me of one of the first stories Peter ever shared with me.

As part of training on microfinance sponsored by the United States Agency for International Development and held in Uganda in 1999, Peter had an opportunity to visit a leading MFI. The MFI was well known as a Christian nonprofit organization and was funded in large part by believers in the U.S. Peter found that it used the same methodology and same loan products as a secular MFI working in the area. The more he compared the two organizations, the less he could find any meaningful difference in their services or relationships with borrowers. Neither one demonstrated Christian discipleship or extraordinary care for employees' or clients' physical, emotional, or spiritual needs. What difference, if any, did being called a Christian organization make? Was it anything more than a fund-raising tool targeting good-hearted and unsuspecting Christian supporters? Unfortunately, there are many so-called faith-based organizations that would be equally hard-pressed to differentiate themselves from secular programs.

When I talk with others about this topic, I illustrate the different nonprofit organizations and churches this way. Assume you have a big dial in front of you. On the far left side is an organization that does an excellent job of helping others but has no desire to share the gospel or represent

Christ. In the left-center of the dial are organizations that intend to share the love of God by helping people but do not intend to make verbal presentations of the gospel unless specifically asked. Their employees may not even be Christians. In the right-center of the dial are organizations that expend their resources to both share the gospel verbally and do some kind of physical relief or development program. On the far right of the dial are evangelistic organizations that almost exclusively share the gospel verbally.

On the left side of this dial, where (if anywhere) might you cease to support an organization if sharing the love of Christ and giving glory to God are important to you? On the right side of the dial, where might you cease to support an organization if helping people both physically and spiritually is important to you? How you answer these two questions should help you choose organizations to support. I have found that my answer (I'm in the center to right-center) is radically different from that of many people.

In dealing with the two sides of the dial, there is a subtle difference. It is fairly simple to see what "good works" organizations are doing. After all, those things are discussed clearly and openly. The same is not true when it comes to helping people spiritually. It can be very difficult to determine somebody's level of witness for the Lord, especially when faraway people have such varying opinions on what it means to witness for the Lord. If verbal sharing of the gospel is important to you, then you should take special care to get a clear understanding of any nonprofit organization or church's intentions and track record in that regard.

Brian Fikkert, director of the Chalmers Center for Economic Development, once told me, "Christian development work must include a clear presentation of the gospel. Failure to do so denies the poor access to the only real solution to the fundamental causes of poverty." It might sound like an obvious starting point, but unless an organization takes significant care to have a corporate culture that emphasizes effective witness for Christ, it will not happen consistently. Granted, individuals in any organization

have an opportunity to act as witnesses for Jesus. However, consistent and reliable acts of witness happen only when the organization's management insists that they happen.

All of the above is not meant to criticize any organization that helps people or shares the gospel. In fact, as I will show below, I think it is a wonderful idea to access these organizations for their services or expertise and even to partner with them in the right circumstances. However, since we all have limited resources, we givers should be careful to use our resources to support those organizations that consistently act in accordance with our own calling and purpose.

There are other organizational characteristics to consider as we decide where to direct our time, energy, and money.

LOCAL CHURCH

Sammy Mah, the president of World Relief, regularly talks about the importance of focusing on "the Big K," the "Kingdom of God." Organizations often spend far too much time building their own little kingdoms and missing the bigger picture. More service could be accomplished if no one cared who gets the credit.

Within this partnership, the indigenous local church must be central. In a small group setting in conjunction with the Peace Plan launch, Rick Warren spoke about the "NGO-ization" of ministry that has replaced the role of the local church. He is largely right. The local church has not been intimately involved in many Christian development projects around the world, much to the detriment of the local church — and to the detriment of the projects. Working with the local church is not easy, yet this church is, and always will be, Christ's body on earth to whom he entrusts the task of feeding the poor and clothing the naked.

No organization is better placed than the local church for providing and administering social services. The local church has the mandate, the credibility, and the connections that yield the most efficient results. By working with a local church, outsiders can take advantage of local resources without appearing to be the source of every solution to every problem. This allows solutions to be locally owned and for local churches to be empowered. The result is longer-term growth and stability.

Helping a local church provide social services also helps it gain the opportunity to share the gospel with people who might not otherwise hear the good news. This allows the local church to develop an integrated ministry of meeting people's financial and spiritual needs.

A common hindrance to working with the local church is the lack of reliable local leadership. Sometimes the solution, rather than turning away, is to raise up and train local leaders. This training might involve theological education, lifestyle modeling, and meeting whatever other specific needs exist. Unfortunately, this takes years of effort so other projects may need to be delayed until this can be accomplished. If a project needs to bypass local Christian leaders, it is a danger sign. When Western organizations find themselves in combat with local leaders, it may be a sign that the Western organization is on shaky ground since locals often understand the situation best. On the other hand, it may also be a sign that local leadership is only protecting its turf and needs to be worked with carefully.

WORKS WELL WITH OTHERS

All programs and churches have limited resources. Whenever it doesn't compromise the mission of the program or church, leveraging the assets of other organizations should be considered. In a small village in the Dominican Republic, I walked by a nicer-than-normal hut with a smiling young woman standing in the doorway. An hour later I walked by again, and she was still standing there and smiling. When I asked my host about her situation, I was told the aid organization that employed this young health worker had mostly solved a particular health care situation in that area. They kept her employed even though she had little work to do. As a result, she now spent most of her day standing in the doorway even though neighboring communities desperately needed her expertise. What was needed was a partnership between this local aid organization and neighboring ones in order to best provide for the needs of the greatest number of people.

Esperanza, a microfinance organization in the Dominican Republic, was astute enough to observe that many charities and governmental agencies provide numerous services throughout the island, many of which go unused because few poor people outside of the local community know about them. Esperanza now learns about all services on the island so they can make them known and available to their clients. At virtually no cost to Esperanza, its clients are accessing a plethora of additional services.

Partnering with secular agencies is an important issue. As long as the Christian organization is transparent about its core goals and beliefs, there are many bridge-building opportunities. As more and more Christian organizations gain reputations for operational excellence, an increasing number of development professionals will seek them out for collaboration.

MEASURE RESULTS

Management guru Peter Drucker said, "You get what you measure."[12] If an organization's goal is to see lasting spiritual fruit, then it is important to find indicators that help steer toward more effective programming. Measuring spiritual indicators needs to be done carefully and comprehensively, just as you measure financial indicators. For instance, the Center for Community Transformation (CCT) has a stated goal of seeing 5 percent of people in the areas where they serve as devoted followers of Jesus Christ and serving as agents of change. The organization measures second-generation disciples, meaning people who have become Christians through the clients who became Christians.

It is frustrating that many nonprofit organizations aren't interested in knowing their effectiveness, either financially or spiritually. The ones who do publish numbers often measure things that are not terribly important. If you choose to support an organization, make sure you understand what kind of results you can expect to see reported and how those results are measured.

The primary reason to calculate cost efficiency is to wisely steward the resources God provides to accomplish his will as best as we understand it. Without establishing standards and measuring results, there is no standard by which to allocate resources to different programs. This is especially important for churches, since the programs they get involved with require long-term commitments. Without proper communication about expectations, it is likely that problems will result.

However, determining and monitoring the correct measures is often exceptionally difficult, especially when spiritual effects are considered. When considering financial results, there are many organizations that attempt to measure and compare the effectiveness of various charities and nonprofit organizations. For the microfinance industry, Mix Market is one of the best. It's a Web-based information platform linking MFIs worldwide with investors and donors in order to promote greater investment and information flow. With a platform for fair and standardized reporting, organizations and individuals around the world have a convenient way to share information with donors and like-minded organizations. In turn, investors and donors can more easily compare MFIs with others of its kind to decide where money will best be used to serve the poor. Mix Market provides data on 1,349 MFIs, 103 investor funds, and 180 partners, or market facilitators.[13]

THE KEY ROLE OF DONORS

History reminds us that the church's involvement in missions and acts of compassion swings like a pendulum. When acts of compassion replace the presentation of the gospel story, the next tendency is to swing to the other extreme and ignore the scriptural commands to serve and love through deeds. The greatest threat to the church's full embrace of this new entrepreneurial approach to integrated word-and-deed missions is the slow compromise of the incorporation of the gospel message. Donors have a key role in protecting this aspect of an organization's mission and preventing this drift from occurring.

CELEBRATING WITH GOATS

(PETER)

After a twenty-four-hour journey from Washington, DC, to Lubumbashi, Congo, missions committee members from Willowdale Chapel and I strapped the seatbelts of a Toyota Land Cruiser for a brain-rattling journey to a small village named Lubanda. Lubanda is located near Congolese mines that are infamous for extracting diamonds and coltanite — the mineral that is used in cell phones and PlayStations. It's ironic, seeing that there isn't even cell phone coverage in Lubanda.

We were visiting this village because of a man affectionately called Monsieur L'Abbey. In this small village that didn't have indoor plumbing or electricity, Monsieur L'Abbey seemed to be a fountain of contagious joy. His tattered white frock matched his wrinkled but exuberant smile. The spring in his step made him seem taller than his five-foot-five stature. When he welcomed our small team at his small brick church, he stated, "Today is a very special day for Lubanda. Thank you for coming."

With grand fanfare in front of the village chief and hundreds of children, Monsieur L'Abbey said their village wanted to provide us with a gift. Four village elders appeared from the side of the building carrying two grown goats, feet tied and bleating uncontrollably. The elders handed me one of the goats and I held it awkwardly, trying to show my gratefulness for this special gift and masking my uneasiness in holding a squirming goat.

In Lubanda, goats cost around $50. There was no doubt that this was sacrificial giving. Village members were obviously among the 80 percent of Congo who live on less than $1 per day. As if this gift were not enough, we entered Monsieur L'Abbey's home where our hands were washed in a small bucket as an elderly woman poured water from a plastic cup as the faucet. This cup became her drinking cup moments later. We ate fufu — the kasava-based staple — rice, and chicken, and drank pineapple soda.

Why such a warm welcome? Why such sacrificial giving? And why such joy?

Monsieur L'Abbey knew that our visit to Lubanda marked the beginning of a new partnership. HOPE International was beginning to provide $50 loans and biblically based education to entrepreneurs in the village. He knew that these loans and training had the potential to radically change lives and alleviate severe poverty. He knew that these services would be

a tangible demonstration and verbal proclamation of a God who sees and responds to the poor.

As we walked around his village, I pressed him for why he believed these loans were going to have such a positive impact on his village. I questioned why he was so grateful that we were beginning operations in Lubanda.

His response was simple: "I know this will help our people."

The more we spoke, the more I saw joy in his life — that mysterious joy that defies circumstance. Joy in giving. Joy in serving. Joy in believing that tomorrow has the potential to be better than today. Joy that flowed

from a relationship with his Creator. Joy in a place that you might not expect to find it. His joy overflowed to his community and to our small group of invited guests.

Receiving a goat and eating fufu with our hands were unforgettable. But the greatest gift Monsieur L'Abbey lavishly gave us was his example of how joy, dignity, and deep satisfaction can be found and shared — even in the most unlikely places.

This evidence of joy is just one more example of why we passionately believe that SCAs, MFIs, and other employment-based solutions are working. They work because they unlock the potential of the poor. They work because they empower entrepreneurs to make a difference in their communities. They work because a hand up is better than a handout. They work because they foster lasting relationships through which physical and spiritual poverty can be seamlessly addressed. And they work because they produce joy and dignity, antidotes to dependency and despair.

Given these tools, the last remaining question is whether we — Western Christians and the Western church — are going to use them. We are optimistic that this generation will move beyond complacency and good intentions to thoughtful action that will have lasting results. And we hope that in so doing, the church will be marked by humility and gratitude for the opportunity to be a part of such an important global mission of seeing the poor become glad.

SELECTED RESOURCES

INTEGRATION OF SPIRITUAL AND PHYSICAL POVERTY

Kingdom Business by David R. Befus

The Lost Art of Discipleship by LeRoy Eims

Transformation: How Glocal Churches Transform Lives and the World by Bob Roberts Jr.

Walking with the Poor by Bryant L. Myers

God Is at Work by Ken Eldred

HOPE Lives by Amber Van Schooneveld

When Charity Destroys Dignity by Glenn Schwartz

Good News to the Poor by Tim Chester

The Chalmers Center for Economic Development, *www.chalmers.org*

MICROFINANCE AND SCAs

A Billion Bootstraps by Phil Smith and Eric Thurman

The Poor and Their Money by Stuart Rutherford

Banker to the Poor by Muhammad Yunus

CGAP, *www.cgap.org*

The Mix Market, *www.mixmarket.org*

The Microfinance Gateway, *www.microfinancegateway.org*

Microcredit Summit, *www.microcreditsummit.org*

POVERTY

The White Man's Burden by William Easterly

The Bottom Billion by Paul Collier

The Rise of Global Civil Society by Don Eberly

World Bank, *www.worldbank.org*

ABOUT
THE PHOTOGRAPHER

Jeremy Cowart is a graphic designer turned photographer from Nashville, Tennessee. As a full-time photographer for only four years, Jeremy specializes in travel, entertainment, reportage, and portrait photography. His clients include ABC, FOX, A&E, FX, Universal Music, Sony Music, and Warner Bros. Records. In 2006 Jeremy released his first book, *Hope in the Dark*.

Jeremy Cowart's pictures are descriptive of the places and people described in this book. With a few exceptions, they are not the actual people or places referenced. He took these pictures on trips with HOPE International, Blood:Water Mission, and the Passion Tour World Tour.

ACKNOWLEDGMENTS

We never really paid much attention to a book's acknowledgments until writing this book. It always seemed like a list of names that we'd rarely recognize. After going through the writing process, we now know how important those names are! Truly, this book was written with the support and encouragement of so many friends, just a few of which receive special mention here.

Jeremy Cowart has been a very special blessing. His photographic skills are surpassed only by his compassion. We also thank Jena Lee Nardella of Blood:Water and Louie Giglio of Passion Tour for allowing the use of pictures Jeremy captured while traveling with their outstanding organizations.

Our sincere thanks go to Rob Bell, not only for his foreword and endorsement of this book, but for consistently and creatively being an advocate for the poor and the power of microfinance.

We were fortunate to end up with the very best associate publisher and agent in the business — Angela Scheff and Greg Daniel, respectively. Zondervan further blessed us by providing editor Becky Philpott, and Tom Dean and his excellent marketing staff.

Josh Kwan, Kevin Panicker, and Mark Russell provided special help in organizing our thoughts and challenging our assumptions. Eric Thurman has been a mentor and example to both of us. Without his willingness to introduce us many years ago, this book would not have happened. Paul and Cindy Marty, Andre Barkov, Carlos Pimentel Sanchez, and Ruth Callanta have given us special inspiration as they continually find innovative ways to offer microfinance services and live in ways that point people toward Jesus.

Mama Monique, Oleg, Musadidi, Milan, Iva, Jose Luis, and the millions of other entrepreneurs who are bringing transformation to your communities, you inspire and motivate us to do more.

PETER

Special thanks goes to all my friends and team members at HOPE International, particularly Justin Bredeman, Jesse Casler, Micah Crist, Beth Goodman, Jill Heisey, Chris Horst, Nate Hulley, Rachel Lapp, Quenton Marty, Katie Nienow, Brenna O'Brien, Sarah Rutt, Katie Straight, Kevin Tordoff, and Jason Williams, "the intern extraordinaire," who provided specific help with this book. I could not imagine working with a more passionate or gifted team. Jeff Rutt and the entire Board, thank you for your enthusiastic support of this project and for giving me the privilege of serving with HOPE.

Dave Larson, your fingerprints are all over this. Thanks for all you taught me about microfinance and keeping the gospel central. David Weekley, Rusty Walter, Terry Looper, George Lindahl, Wil VanLoh, Jeff Hildebrand, Tiger Dawson, and John Montgomery — your support, mentoring, and Dominican Republic trips are legendary. Thank you! The Homes for Hope team deserves special recognition, as do my very special friends, John and Jacque Weberg. Your selfless giving is an inspiration and encouragement that has touched millions. David Butler, Alan Barnhart, Jim Bisenius, Andy Crouch, Chris Crane, Dabbs Calvin, Greg Campbell, Jim Deitch, Don Eberly, Todd Engelsen, Marlin Horst, Todd Hendricks, Henry Kaestner, Kurt Keilhacker, Gabe Lyons, Doug McClay, Roy Millender, Rick Oppenheimer, Lyston Peebles, Jeff Sandefer, Fred Smith, Ron Thompson, Bill Townsend, Michael Tremain, Baxter Underwood, Chuck Waterfield, and Greg Watts have come alongside me at just the right time and in just the right way.

Mom and Dad, thanks for living out what it means to authentically follow Jesus. I think you owe me Kimball's. To the rest of my family — I still can't believe you were willing to read a draft while on vacation at Raystown Lake. Thank you!

Laurel, Keith, Liliana, and Myles — you are the joys and loves of my life. Thank you for being so encouraging of this project and making home a place I always can't wait to get to. Love you!

This book was largely written on planes and in airports. Special thanks to every Southwest flight attendant who provided as many peanuts as I could eat. The soundtrack for writing was Switchfoot, U2, and Bebo Norman.

PHIL

Special thanks to Shannon for giving up hundreds of hours we could have shared together, and to Laura and Mom, for editing my scribbles over the last two years.

There are simply too many people to mention who have endured my trial balloons, but Mariann McKinney, Bill Dozier, J. D. Payne, Dave McCabe, Ken Albright, Larry Christian, Larry Akers, and Don Millican deserve special crowns. My special spiritual mentors John Barnett, Mitch Wilburn, Mark Moore, and Bruce Ewing have been patient beyond belief.

Soli Deo Gloria.
Peter Greer
Phil Smith

NOTES

INTRODUCTION: GLIMPSES OF POVERTY

1. Conversation at Discovery Church, Orlando, Fla., February 26, 2008.

2. In 2008 Urwego changed its name to Urwego Opportunity Bank and is now jointly owned by World Relief, World Relief Canada, HOPE International, and Opportunity International. Since the references to Urwego in this book precede the merger, its original name, Urwego, is used throughout this book.

CHAPTER 1: FLOWER PETALS IN THE FACE

1. Name changed for security.

2. Hari Kumar and Heather Timmons, "Violence in India Is Fueled by Religious and Economic Divide," *New York Times on the Web*, September 3, 2008, *www.nytimes.com/2008/09/04/world/asia/04christians.html?pagewanted=1&r=1&ei=5070&emc=eta1* (September 7, 2008).

3. Geography IQ, "Infant Mortality Rate," *www.geographyiq.com/ranking/ranking_Infant_Mortality_Rate_aall.htm* (August 19, 2008).

4. University of Texas Health Science Center at Houston, "Novel Compound May Treat Acute Diarrhea," *Science Daily*, June 21, 2008, *www.sciencedaily.com/releases/2008/06/080616170801.htm* (August 19, 2008).

5. International Literacy Day, *www.sil.org/literacy/litfacts.htm* (November 18, 2008).

6. *The CIA World Factbook*, "Afghanistan," *www.cia.gov/library/publications/the-world-factbook/print/af.html* (August 19, 2008).

7. Mark Kinver, "Water Policy 'Fails World's Poor,'" BBC News on the Web, March 9, 2006, *http://news.bbc.co.uk/2/hi/science/nature/4787758.stm* (August 19, 2008).

8. *The CIA World Factbook*, "USA," *www.cia.gov/library/publications/the-world-factbook/geos/us.html* (August 19, 2008).

9. *The CIA World Factbook*, "Swaziland," *www.cia.gov/library/publications/the-world-factbook/geos/wz.html* (August 19, 2008).

10. Kirk Magelby, "MicroFranchises as a Solution to Global Poverty," December 2005, *www.microfranchises.org/file.php?id=35* (August 19, 2008).

11. Even though by global standards there are few poor people in America, there *are* real needs all around us. The poverty that exists in the U.S. still causes pain and hopelessness. The church must be engaged in bringing hope and healing to the physical, emotional, and spiritual needs in our own backyards and neighboring cities. In no way do we desire to dissuade engagement and service or overlook the poor in America, for there is still so much more to do. Rather, our desire is to argue for a "both/and" approach that sees needs in the U.S. but does not overlook the needs in other forgotten parts of the world.

12. "The Mountain Man and the Surgeon," *The Economist*, December 20, 2005, *www.econ.umn.edu/~wiseman/1102s07/mountain.pdf* (August 19, 2008).

13. For a more complete analysis of the breakdown of poverty and the difference between the countries moving out of poverty and those stuck in a poverty trap, we recommend *The Bottom Billion: Why the Poorest Countries Are Failing and What Can Be Done About It* by Paul Collier (Oxford: Oxford University Press, 2007).

14. One more disclaimer: It is exceedingly dangerous to write about "the poor," "the developing world," or "people in poverty," for in each of these categories are individuals who are anything but homogeneous. Only reluctantly do we use these gross generalizations in this book to highlight overall trends. We must never forget that individuals living in poverty are individuals; there are no "average" people. Each person has a name, a mother, a father, and their own story. Each has emotions, dreams, and desires. God made each one with the same care that he used in making each and every one of us. It is appropriate that we should consider every one of them our neighbor.

15. Quote from a presentation given at PEER Servants' Ricchari Conference in Peru, August 2, 2007.

CHAPTER 2: MAKING A FEAST FOR JESUS

1. Special thanks to Keith Greer for his insights on the early church, historical examples, and great reversal.

2. Rodney Stark, *The Rise of Christianity: A Sociologist Reconsiders History* (Princeton, NJ: Princeton University Press, 2006), 1.

3. J. Wesley Bready, *England: Before & After Wesley* (New York: Harper & Brothers, 1940), 14.

4. Samuel Escobar and John Driver, *Introduction to Christian Mission & Social Justice* (Scottsdale, Penn.: Herald Press, 1978), 7 – 9.

5. Walter Rauschenbusch, *A Theology of the Social Gospel* (New York: Macmillan, 1917), 145.

6. Bryant L. Myers, *Walking with the Poor* (New York: Orbis, 2006), 6.

7. Americans are notorious for significantly overestimating the amount of funding governments actually provide in international aid and in personal charity. Consider the following information on how much countries actually contribute per person.

	Aid through taxes, per person	Aid through charities, per person
Australia	$92	$31
Canada	$110	$34
France	$164	n/a
Germany	$123	$16
Ireland	$207	$82
Italy	$74	$2
Japan	$98	$2
Netherlands	$319	$17
Norway	$592	n/a
Sweden	$397	$1
United Kingdom	$190	$9
United States	$85	$30

Giles Bolton, *Africa Doesn't Matter* (New York: Arcade, 2008), 88.

8. Mark Russell, "The Use of Business in Missions in Chiang Mai, Thailand," PhD dissertation (Wilmore, Ky.: Asbury Theological Seminary, 2008). This dissertation concerns missionaries who are involved in business as missions. In the dissertation, Russell contrasts two groups of missionaries. The first group says that their primary goal is to convert people to Christianity. The second group says that they are there to bless the people and to help them in numerous ways, such as finding meaningful employment, restoring relationships, providing for their families, etc. Which of these two groups is more effective in making disciples? Intuition might say the first group since they are not distracted by all the other things that the second group is trying to do. The finding was startling. The second group was more effective in making disciples by a 48 to 1 ratio.

9. David Kinnaman and Gabe Lyons, *UnChristian* (Grand Rapids: Baker, 2007), 65.

10. Kinnaman and Lyons, *UnChristian*, 70. The authors describe the Barna Group's research and how it relates to perceptions about Christians. When born-again Busters (their description) were asked how they came to faith, 71 percent responded that it was the result of a relationship.

CHAPTER 3: SEARCHING FOR SOLUTIONS THAT WORK

1. Jeff Rutt used this experience as his basis to found HOPE International, a global microfinance network.

2. This is not to insinuate that there are not benefits of short-term trips, particularly for the trip participants. Seth Barnes of Adventures in Missions describes that when people "step out of their comfort zones and embrace what God is doing around the world, they do not return the same." Well-orchestrated trips provide an opportunity to awaken men and women to their own American brand of spiritual poverty and show them the difference that a living God at work in their lives and in the lives of the people they meet can make to transform a community. He described some who go on trips as becoming "wrecked for the ordinary" — we celebrate when that is the case. But besides these positive impacts on the participants, we do need to simultaneously examine the impact on the recipients of our charity.

3. Joel Wickre, "Missions That Heal," *Christianity Today*, July 13, 2007, *www.christianitytoday.com/ct/2007/julyweb-only/128 – 52.0.html* (June 20, 2008).

4. Michael M. Phillips, "Unanswered Prayers: In Swaziland, US Preacher Sees His Dream Vanish," *Wall Street Journal*, December 19, 2005.

5. Giles Bolton, *Africa Doesn't Matter* (New York: Arcade, 2008), 76.

6. Bolton, *Africa Doesn't Matter*, 224.

CHAPTER 4: A HAND UP, NOT A HANDOUT

1. Frank M. Loewenberg, *From Charity to Social Justice* (New Brunswick, NJ: Transaction, 2001), 95.

2. Marvin Olasky, *The Tragedy of American Compassion* (Washington, DC: Regnery, 1992), 9.

3. Ibid.

4. Ibid., 142.

5. Ibid., 154.

6. Steve Saint, *The Great Omission: Fulfilling Christ's Commission Completely* (Seattle: YWAM, 2001), 102.

7. *CIA Factbook, www.cia.gov/library/publications/the-world-factbook/geos/cb.html* (November 24, 2008).

CHAPTER 5: UNLOCKING ENTREPRENEURSHIP

1. Nicholas Kristof, "You, Too, Can Be a Banker to the Poor," *The New York Times,* March 27, 2007.

2. Hernando de Soto, *The Mystery of Capital: Why Capitalism Triumphs in the West and Fails Everywhere Else* (New York: Basic Books, 2000), 4.

3. This story is adapted from one told by Stuart Rutherford in *The Poor and Their Money* (New Delhi: Oxford University Press, 2000), 13–20.

4. On average, she has 550 rupees on deposit. 100/550 = 18 percent. Annualized, since she did this for only part of the year, it is 30 percent.

5. Dave Larson, *MED Monday Minute*, Unpublished Newsletter, August 27, 2007.

6. Madeleine Buntang, "Bono Talks of US Crusade," *The Guardian*, June 16, 2005, *www.guardian.co.uk/world/2005/jun/16/g8.usa* (August 20, 2008).

7. Transcript, CNN interview with Rwandan President Paul Kagame, September 17, 2005, *http://transcripts.cnn.com/TRANSCRIPTS/0509/17/i_if.01.html* (August 2008).

CHAPTER 6: A BRASS RING FOR THE POOR

1. Stuart Rutherford, *The Poor and Their Money* (New Delhi: Oxford University Press, 2000), 41.

2. "Stories from the Field," Chalmers Center at Covenant College, undated.

3. Jeffrey Ashe and Elisabeth Rhyne, "Point, Counterpoint: A Dialogue on Member-Owned Financial Institutions and Increasing Access to Savings Facilities," 22 (2005), *www.cgap.org/gm/document–1.9.2118/47623_file_Poor_People_s_Savings_q_As_with_Experts.pdf* (August 16, 2008).

CHAPTER 7: MICROFINANCE GOES MAINSTREAM

1. Srikant M. Datar, Marc J. Epstein, and Kristi Yuthas, "In Microfinance, Clients Must Come First," *Stanford Social Innovation Review*, Winter 2008, 44.

2. Robert Hickson, *http://english.handan.edu.cn/english/2005/Nov/150021.htm* (July 29, 2008).

3. Opportunity International eNewsletter, September 2006.

4. Elizabeth Littlefield, Johnathan Murduch, and Syed Hashemi, "Is Microfinance an Effective Strategy to Reach the Millennium Development Goals?" CGAP Focus Note 24, January 2003, *www.microfinancegateway.org/files/3656_101.htm* (September 9, 2008).

5. "UPS Gives $1 Million to Microlenders as Part of 100th Birthday Celebration," *Transport Topics*, November 12, 2007, 31.

CHAPTER 8: EXPLORING VARIATIONS IN MICROFINANCE 2.0

1. Isobel Coleman, interview by Eben Kaplan, November 8, 2005, *www.cfr.org /publication/9173/microcredit_gaining_momentum_says_councils_isobel_coleman.html* (August 21, 2008).

2. Grameen Phone, September 20, 2007, *www.grameenphone.com/index.php?id=64* (August 11, 2008).

3. Urwego, *www.urwego.org/info/prodservice.html* (July 7, 2008).

4. "Overcoming HIV and Building Her Community," *www.evancarmichael.com /African-Accounts/1678/Overcoming-HIV-and-Building-Her-Community.html* (November 24, 2008).

5. ASPE Issue Brief, "Overview of the Uninsured in the United States: An Analysis of the 2007 Current Population Survey," September 2007, *http://aspe.hhs.gov/health /reports/07/uninsured/index.htm* (August 5, 2008).

6. Opportunity International, "Opportunity International's Micro Insurance Agency to Develop and Provide Life, Health and Crop Insurance for 21 Million Poor People," *www .opportunity.org/NETCOMMUNITY/Page.aspx?pid=458&srcid=265* (August 5, 2008).

7. Micro Insurance Agency, *www.microinsuranceagency.com/about-micro.html* (November 24, 2008).

8. Ibid.

9. Ibid.

10. Freedom from Hunger, "Credit with Education in the Andes," *www.freedomfrom hunger.org/programs/andes.php* (August 12, 2008).

11. Center for Community Transformation, "Serving God by Serving the Poor," *http:// cct.org.ph/microfinance2.php#health* (July 7, 2008).

12. The HealthStore Foundation, "The Micro-Franchising Model — An Effective, Scalable Solution," *http://www.cfwshops.org/overview.html* (July 8, 2008).

13. HealthStore, "The Micro-Franchising Model — A New Way Forward," *http://www .cfwshops.org/model.html* (July 8, 2008).

14. Institute for Women's Policy Research, "Job Training and Education Fight Poverty," IWPR Publication #D444 (April 2002), *http://www.iwpr.org/pdf/d444.pdf* (July 7, 2008).

15. Michael Wines, "Malnutrition Is Cheating Its Survivors, and Africa's Future," New York Times Online, December 28 2006, *www.nytimes.com/2006/12/28/world /africa/28malnutrition.html* (July 7, 2008).

16. Grameen Dialogue, "Grameen Danone Foods Launched," *www.grameen-info.org /dialogue/dialogue63/regularfl2.html* (July 7, 2008).

17. IFAD, "Emerging Lessons in Agricultural Microfinance: Selected Case Studies," 2006, *www.ifad.org/ruralfinance/pub/case_studies.pdf* (August 12, 2008).

18. Agros International, "Who Is Agros?" *www.agros.org/ag/inside-agros/who-is-agros* (August 12, 2008).

19. Agros, *www.agros.org/ag/how-we-work/people-and-progress/* (November 24, 2008).

20. Environmental News Network, "Using Microfinance to Bring Safe Drinking Water to Rural India," March 25, 2008, *www.enn.com/business/article/33516* (August 14, 2008).

21. PBS Foundation, "Q & A with Muhammad Yunus," *www.pbs.org/now/enterprising ideas/Muhammad-Yunus.html* (July 8, 2008).

22. Muhammad Yunus, "Grameen Bank's Struggling (Beggar) Members Programme," July 2005, *www.grameen-info.org/index.php?option=com_content&task=view&id=221&It emid=172* (July 8, 2008).

23. PBS Foundation, "Q & A with Muhammad Yunus," *www.pbs.org/now/enterprising ideas/Muhammad-Yunus.html* (July 8, 2008).

24. YouthWorks, "Empowering Youth through Microfinance and ICT Philippines," 2007, *www.unitarny.org/mm/File/Audrey_Resaved.pdf* (August 12, 2008).

25. Human Rights Watch, "Abuses of Women and Girls That Fuel HIV/AIDS," *www .hrw.org/reports/2003/africa1203/2.htm* (September 7, 2008).

CHAPTER 9: IT CAN'T BE THAT GOOD, CAN IT?

1. Special thanks to Dave Larson for his contributions in this chapter.

2. Muhammad Yunus, interview by Jonathon Gatehouse, November 27, 2006, *www .macleans.ca/world/global/article.jsp?content=20061127_137041_137041* (August 2, 2008).

3. Breaking News English, "Zimbabwe's Homeless Ignored," June 25, 2005, *www .breakingnewsenglish.com/0506/050625-zimbabwe-e.html* (August 2, 2008).

4. Richard Krause, "Anaphylaxis," *www.emedicine.com/emerg/TOPIC25.HTM* (August 11, 2008).

CHAPTER 10: USING THE SECOND-BEST DISTRIBUTION SYSTEM

1. "Stories from the Field," Chalmers Center at Covenant College, undated.

2. Andrew Higgins, "Episcopal Church Dissidents Seek Authority Overseas," *Wall Street Journal*, September 20, 2007, A1.

3. Brian Fikkert, "Christian Microfinance: Which Way Now?" (Working Paper no. 205), Association of Christian Economists, 20th Anniversary Conference, January 2003, 34.

CHAPTER 11: PASTORS SELDOM MAKE GOOD BANKERS

1. Gustav Niebuhr, "Episcopal Dissidents Find African Inspiration," *New York Times*, March 6, 2001, *www.nytimes.com/2001/03/06/national/06FLOR.html?ex=1218168000 &en=c969d59a5617cb9e&ei=5070* (August 6, 2008).

2. Giles Bolton, *Africa Doesn't Matter: How the West Has Failed the Poorest Continent and What We Can Do about It* (New York: Arcade, 2008), 289.

3. Brian Fikkert, "Case Study of the Self-Help Affinity Group Model of the Bunyoro-Kitara Diocese of Anglican Church of Uganda," *www.chalmers.org/site/resources /workpap/Bunyoro_Case_Study_Public.pdf* (September 18, 2008).

4. Ibid.

5. Personal letter from Brian Fikkert to Phil Smith, June 4, 2007.

CHAPTER 13: KEEPING OUR EYES ON THE PRIZE

1. Bolton, *Africa Doesn't Matter*, 140.

2. Tim Dearborn, "Living Our Christian Commitments, Remaining Faithful as a Christian Organization in a Changing World," *Christian Commitments PowerPoint Presentation* (World Vision International), undated.

3. Paul Collier, *The Bottom Billion* (Oxford: Oxford University Press, 2007), 66.

4. Bolton, *Africa Doesn't Matter* (New York: Arcade, 2008), 88.

5. Ibid., 91.

CHAPTER 14: GOD'S BUSINESS

1. David R. Befus, *Kingdom Business* (Miami: Latin American Mission, 2001), 14.

2. Bob Roberts Jr., *Transformation: How Glocal Churches Transform Lives and the World* (Grand Rapids: Zondervan, 2006), 45–46.

3. Chron.com, "Sowing the Seeds of Change in Africa," *www.chron.com/disp/story.mpl /business/5476684.html* (July 22, 2008).

4. Mission Predisan, "Predisan's History," *www.predisan.org/index.php?option=com _content&task=view&id=34* (September 18, 2008).

5. *Christian Post*, vol. 9, no. 2 (June 2007), 8–9.

CHAPTER 15: WAYS TO WORK FOR GOD

1. David R. Befus, *Kingdom Business* (Miami: Latin America Mission, 2001), 16. This is an excellent resource for the details of implementing employment-based solutions.

CHAPTER 16: GOING CORPORATE FOR THE POOR

1. "Business as Mission," Mats Tunehad, Wayne McGee, and Josie Plummer, eds., Lausanne Occasional Paper no. 59 (Lausanne: Lausanne Committee for World Evangelization, 2005), 5.

2. Ibid, 21.

3. Mark Russell, "The Use of Business in Missions in Chiang Mai, Thailand," PhD dissertation (Wilmore, Ky.: Asbury Theological Seminary, 2008), 1, 2.

CHAPTER 17: ROLLING UP OUR SLEEVES

1. Don Miller, *Free Market Jesus* sermon, DVD (Bluefish TV, 2007) *www.bluefishtv.com*.

2. Virb, "Junky Car Club: Living with Less So We Can Give Them More," *http://virb.com/junkycarclub* (August 14, 2008).

3. Ronald Sider, *Rich Christians in an Age of Hunger* (Nashville: Thomas Nelson, 2005).

4. Kay Walsh, *http://www.peerservants.org/volunteers-kay.html* (December 2, 2008).

5. Rick Warren, "Great Commission Eyes," *http://dailyscripturedevotional.com/devotional/great-commission-eyes/* (January 12, 2009).

6. Compassion International, "Compassion Employee's Book 'Hope Lives' offered as Ministry Kits," June 2, 2008, *www.compassion.com/press/currentnews/june–2008-hope-lives-amber-van-schooneveld-compassion-international.htm* (August 22, 2008).

7. *Worldwide Faith News*, "Ecumenical Study Guide on Global Poverty and MDGs," *www.wfn.org/2007/02/msg00085.html* (August 18, 2008).

8. Wikipedia, "Millennium Development Goals," *http://en.wikipedia.org/wiki/Millennium_Development_Goals* (September 18, 2008).

9. Greg Thompson. Personal Interview (December 15, 2008).

10. Abram Huyser Honig, "Study Questions Whether Short-Term Missions Make a Difference," *Christianity Today*, June 20, 2005, *www.christianitytoday.com/ct/2005/juneweb-only/12.0c.html* (August 21, 2008).

11. Penny Project, *www.fumcbirmingham.org/aspcms/youthpennyproject.aspx* (August 21, 2008).

12. Peter Drucker, *The Practice of Management* (New York: Harper & Brothers, 1954).

13. Mix Market, *www.mixmarket.org/en/partners/partners.quick.search.asp* (January 5, 2009).

Join the revolution to lift the world out of poverty.

Go to http://givehope.org